SEVEN INNER JOURNEYS

Also by Ruth White & Mary Swainson
GILDAS COMMUNICATES

RUTH WHITE & MARY SWAINSON

Seven Inner Journeys

LONDON

NEVILLE SPEARMAN

First published in Great Britain in 1974 by
Neville Spearman Limited
112 Whitfield Street, London W1P 6DP

ISBN 0 85435 312 7

Set in 11pt Baskerville 1½pt leaded
and printed and bound by The Garden City Press Limited,
Letchworth, Hertfordshire, SG6 1JS.
Dalmore paper supplied by Frank Grunfeld Ltd.,
London.

For those
who go upon a journey

ACKNOWLEDGEMENTS

We are grateful to all who have helped us to bring out this book: Gildas' many readers who have called it forth; Phoebe Carter and Dorothy Pockley for work with the text; John Read for his friendship and constructively critical support over the years; and those unnamed friends who have shared their own inner journeys.

Our thanks are also due to Messrs Faber and Faber for permission to quote from different parts of *The Cocktail Party* by T. S. Eliot, and to the Editor of *Light* for allowing us to reproduce passages from 'The Seamy Side of Aquarius' by Gildas.

CONTENTS

FOREWORD

By John Read, M.R.C.S., L.R.C.P.; L.D.S.

In 1958 Mary Swainson asked me to give my professional opinion on the mental state of one of the students who was coming to her for psychological counselling. It so happened that Mary Swainson and I, quite independently and unknown to one another, had started Services of this kind for College students; I from a psychiatric basis at the Maudsley Hospital and the London School of Economics, she as a Lecturer in Education at Leicester with an educational and lay-therapeutic point of view. By this time we had become friends, and so, when she was in some doubt whether this particular student was heading for a severe and possibly incurable mental derangement, she turned to me as one likely from my own experience to know as much about student mental health as anyone. The oddness of the main symptom, if such it could be called, was the reason for asking my advice. According to my own memory, the student who had consulted Mary Swainson because, among other difficulties, she was suffering from a progressive, undiagnosed deterioration of vision (which was threatening the poor girl with early blindness) told Mary, when she felt confident enough to do so, that she was aware of a person, apparently a man, not visible to other people, who was her frequent companion and who advised and helped her in the manner of a guardian angel. This student was Ruth.

The notes made at our interview I destroyed when I retired three years ago. I have not met Ruth since. I remember her as a brown-haired girl of medium height, quietly dressed, with nothing in the least eccentric about her either in appearance or manner. She was reserved but not withdrawn and she co-operated quite calmly in our interview which followed a fairly usual psychiatric pattern. I detected none of the oddities of

9

speech or manner that could justify a tentative diagnosis of schizophrenia, which I imagine some conventional psychiatrists might have been inclined to attach to their report. When asked about Gildas, she admitted his existence without hesitation. When I asked if he were present, she said that he was. When I asked where, she pointed to my couch which was near her left side. I felt rather foolish as I was quite unaware of any other presence in my room; but this could have been as much due to my insensitiveness as to the delusion of my patient. It would be as foolish to deny the omnipresence of wireless waves because, without receiving apparatus, we cannot hear any messages, or to declare that there are no such things as bacteria because our eyes are not microscopes.

So I wrote to Mary that, while I did not understand what Gildas might be, I saw no evidence of schizophrenia or anything of that kind.

This was near the beginning of Mary's and Ruth's friendship. It is a pleasant thought that what I said then may have been reassuring and that their partnership led to the productive results which have been reported in *Gildas Communicates*.

Gildas, Mary and Ruth had nearly equal shares in *Gildas Communicates*. This book is Ruth's. For although the other two contribute importantly, it is Ruth's spiritual adventures, as she struggles painfully towards her initiations, which are its core.

The book is dedicated to 'Those who go upon a journey' to encourage them against the doubts and fears that may beset them; but it can appeal to, interest and instruct others of us who are not aware consciously that we are doing any such thing. It may serve to turn our minds in a new and fertile direction. Too long in this period of intense materialism have we been preoccupied with what most people would declare to be the concrete realities of life. But the physical world is beginning to turn into an uninteresting cage. Even in my short life we have seen the most remarkable extension of the physical possibilities available to us. Technological progress and progress in the means of transport have put the four corners of the world within our reach, if we are prepared to go to a little trouble. But this is an equivocal benefit. When I was a boy, adventures within the geographical world seemed to be without bounds. Tropical forests, deserts or arctic wastes were so far beyond my likely purview that my fantasies could disport themselves there indefinitely. Now, with all parts of the world discovered and explored and most of them quite frequently visited, there is less and less magic in fancying oneself here or there and, alas, even in going there oneself. Even the effort of climbing Everest does not seem to be worth the trouble and danger; for our intuitions tell us that, unless to be so positioned in space evokes for symbolic reasons a profound response in our interior spiritual nature, then the whole project will be relatively fruitless. Even the miracles of space travel, which are certainly beyond the resources of the great majority of us, evoke very little imaginative response from us, as we know that the space into which we should be projected by these means would indeed be, for us, empty.

In actual fact the great adventures of material discovery were practical in intention and result : sea-faring voyages to discover better ways of bringing home the treasures of the East; journeys across the New World to find gold and emeralds in Peru. The manifest purpose of these Inner Journeys, so lovingly supported at the this-world level by Mary, was to prepare and train Ruth to be a responsible, reliable and dedicated sensitive for mediumship.

The Journeys had a redemptive purpose for Ruth herself, which explains why some of the experiences she encountered were so very painful; but, as Mary points out in Chapter 13, they affect issues greater than her personal destiny, as Gildas indicates when she is preparing for the fourth Journey. Could it be that, with suitable preparation and under careful guidance, those of the necessary endowment might undertake such journeys as these, much as the contemplative religious devote their lives to selfless intercessory prayer? I think it may be so. But whether or not we feel equal to embark on Inner Journeys such as these, we can all benefit by listening to the profoundly good advice that the Angel gave to Ruth which is recorded at the beginning of Chapter Three.

Those of us who think that we know something about depth psychology may be tempted to fit interpretations to these adventures; but we shall narrow our experience by so doing, for we shall most likely be fitting the incidents in this narrative into our own favourite system and so limit the richness of our response. Mary's theoretical commentary in Chapters one and thirteen is quite sufficient and very clear. My own feeling is that we should try as best we can to go with Ruth on these journeys as we read about them and to learn what we can by our imaginative response.

Tobermory, 7.4.74.

PREFACE

By Mary

'Gildas,' Ruth asked, as long ago as 1959, 'what do you think of the idea that we should one day write a book? Would we have your permission?'

'Yes, Ruth, most willingly. Provided that such a book were written in the right spirit of humility, as I am sure it would be, it could be a valuable contribution to a troubled world. But the time is not yet ready for this kind of writing; men are not yet in tune with the Infinite. There are those who listen but cannot hear, who look but cannot see; those who hear without understanding, those who see without comprehension; but many more whose eyes and ears of the spirit are blind and deaf. One day there will be a reawakening of men's souls, and their re-created minds will encompass gladly great spiritual values. All this, of course, takes a very long time, but you may be assured that the time is not so far distant when the publication of experiences like yours will find acceptance, and will help to fulfil a spiritual need. So you may be assured that when the time comes you will have my every blessing on the work of publication.'

Now, fifteen years later, when the Changes are in progress; when material values are crumbling; when the individual, the country, and the world are passing through a period of chaos and major transformation: this seems to us the right time. Gildas has said:

'On every front, at every level, the battle of good and evil must go on, and the way to victory is through transmutation. The evil must be allowed to manifest, to come near to the light, and thus be changed itself *into* light. Only when the evil is pushed into the darkness can it gain more power.'

Further, transmutation on a personal scale parallels that on a world scale—indeed often precedes it:

13

'That with which you struggle in your own lives is but a reflection of what is being done for the world . . . That which you achieve is mirrored and magnified and forms part of the great throbbing force of light and positive life which will be the saving of the world.'

The last two passages are taken from our first book *Gildas Communicates* (Spearman, 1971). Because these communications take the form of general teachings aimed at preparing us all for the Changes, we were advised to bring them out first.

Seven Inner Journeys, however, is a more specific study. Chronologically preceding the other book, it tells of Ruth's own development and preparation for her work in the field of redemption and regeneration—a task which lasted intensively for eleven years and which still continues.

Although it is a continuous story—almost a saga—we have attempted to preserve its integrity as true experience by presenting the records as they were written at the time of—or in some instances a few weeks or months after—the actual happenings. Some authors have converted their inner experiences into novel form, but this is a *documentary* : fact not fiction. And we hope that it may be of use as one example in a collection of 'journal material' for possible future research, as the New Age comes into being.

Researchers in psychological and psychic fields have asked for an account of 'the emergence of Gildas' in Ruth's consciousness. They will find it in this book. At first she refers to him as 'the angel', but when she knows him better he tells her that he is on the human line of evolution; he is her 'perfect partner', having incarnated sometimes with, sometimes without her; in her present life he is acting as her inner guide and teacher.

His final incarnation, he told her, was in a warm and sunny part of France during the fourteenth century; this was a simple and beautiful life in which there was a perfect balance between earth and heaven. Since then, he has no longer any need to incarnate, although, he says, he still remains subject to similar laws of learning, and must endeavour to progress from plane to plane. His name, Gildas, is pronounced in the French fashion, with a very soft G, as is the French J in 'Je' : 'Jildass'. It means

'The Messenger of Truth', and was quite a common name, he says, in fourteenth-century France. He denies any connection with the early mediaeval historian—or with any other famous personage—of that name. In fact, he discourages questions about details of former lives, preferring to save time and power for teaching; yet he assures us that when the Changes come fully we shall see and know these things directly for ourselves.

Ruth sees him with her 'inner eyes' and hears him with her 'inner ears'. She sees him dressed (usually) in a loose, white, monkish robe. He is very tall, dark, with a young-looking face, and his expression is full of radiance and compassion. His eyes (though once, in fun, he described them as yellow) are a luminous pale brown in colour, and he has a deep, mellow voice, full of gentle humour.

This description is given so that readers may be able to imagine Gildas more realistically. As our awareness increases, and the 'veil' thins, we work more and more closely with these people on the 'other side', finding how natural and normal this relationship can be. So this book is presented in the hope that it may be a comfort and encouragement to many others who have similar experiences; those who, perhaps, face parallel tests and ordeals in darkness, with corresponding joys of light, in their inner lives. In the past, so many have felt 'different' and alone in this type of experience; but, as the New Age comes to birth, they will realize that they are among the pioneers.

If the Aquarian age is one of violence and 'seaminess' on every level (and it will be worked out on every level—within individual personalities, in personal, national, and international relationships) it is also an age of birth or re-birth. The violent pangs which will take place are the pangs which will bring about a new birth of the spirit—again on every level. The birth or re-birth of spirit at the individual level is already being experienced by more and more people each day, and these are the people to whom we speak with a firm and continual message of hope, peace and joy . . .

The most important and lasting lessons of life are learned in the blackest depths, and it is the jewel brought forth from darkness which is the eventual strength of the individual or the nation. Out of the darkness—the horror—the violence—shall be born love, light and joy.

Gildas (from 'The Seamy Side of Aquarius', *Light*, March, 1973.)

CHAPTER 1

What are Inner Journeys?

By Mary

As we rise again from the trough of materialism which characterized the last two or three centuries, more and more people (especially, it would seem, the young) are registering experiences in other dimensions of consciousness—other orders of being—and at varying levels.

Mad or Sane?

By some authorities such experiences are regarded as hallucinations and delusions, and indeed there may well be only a thin line between a significant pattern, on the one hand, and a meaningless dazzle (like a television screen imperfectly tuned) on the other. The major criteria for health in this field, I would suggest, are :

(1) The consistency, and often the continuity, of the experiences.
(2) The degree of stability and strength of the conscious ego, which maintains throughout the freedom of choice and decision-making, never being compulsively 'invaded' by the unconscious beyond control.
(3) The ability to integrate the insights gained with here-and-now living, applying them sensibly and wisely in self-education without inflation.

Those who become unbalanced—carried away by powers which they cannot understand—will indeed find themselves suffering from a 'break-down' (which yet may be respected and used as a healing crisis) when the experiences may have to be controlled by tranquillizing drugs and even hospitalization. But, as trained mystics, most Jungian psychotherapists, and all those who meditate wisely know, the wisdom of the 'inner world', if rightly understood and applied, can be of the utmost benefit in bringing basic meaning and value into all that we do and are in the 'field-work' of daily life. In Ruth's case, she saw a first-rate psychiatrist, at my request, early in the course of the work; he reported that he could find no trace of psychosis.

The so-called "hallucinogenic' (mind-opening) drugs are not necessary for this exploration, although some have found them a useful initial—though an inadequate and potentially dangerous —way in. They were certainly never taken by Ruth, nor by any others who have done 'inner journey' work with me. Some people are innately more able to 'shift level' and to find the inner way congenial than are others. As one young man (aged twenty at the time and reading for a degree in Sociology) wrote while on an inner journey, 'I was aware that my experience was not the only possible one, but it was the truth for me. Others find fulfilment in varying ways; for me it was the inward road. I knew many people for whom I could see that this inward experience of the mind was fulfilment but who were searching as yet in the dark. I could but offer hope and encouragement in telling of others who had taken this path, for the answer lay yet within themselves. This seems to frighten many people; they had indeed lost their 'souls', and the soul's existence was denied by society; yet my mention of the world within made them wary, as if they were deliberately trying to suppress something.'

The response of the general public to phenomena perceived through expanded awareness depends to a considerable extent on the mode of presentation—the idiom. (Here one needs to walk very warily, not only because of in-built prejudice, but because of the valid difference of personality-type among readers, so that a 'multi-lingual' form of communication is desirable!) Thus some, who can take Science Fiction and UFOs in their stride, yet regard the dynamic images of poetry as 'airy-fairy'; to others the 'jargon' of Theosophy, Anthroposophy, or Spiritualism is unacceptable, yet they may well find equivalent feeling-insights through the media of drama, music, dance and ritual. To many, 'psychology' is a 'bad word'; 'religion' is seen as 'outdated'; in communicating with some groups one has to search for the current 'in' phraseology in order to mediate the timeless, central truths. So, to write an introduction to a book on inner journeys is not easy, but I shall endeavour to approach the subject from at least four angles, hoping to offend as few as possible.

Traditional Wisdom, the Ancient Mysteries, Literature

I can only touch on this vast field, but those who have studied at least a little Anthropology, Mythology, Folk Wisdom, and in particular the Sagas, Mysteries, and Initiations of India, Tibet, Egypt, Ancient Greece and many other even older civilizations, will have met most of the universal, archetypal symbols, tests and ordeals. They will realize that people in the past were often closer to the inner consciousness—and more at home with the interplay between inner and outer—than we are now. (It is as if we had gone far out into the lonely isolation of a rigidly classified diversity, and were only now beginning to return and to know that all is one.) For these so-called 'inner' experiences were as 'real' to those undergoing the trials and initiations as our outer world is to us today, indeed probably more so. We have tended to interpret the fuller in terms of the more restricted grades of significance, 'explaining away' pregnant symbols as mere signs or even as amusing customs and superstitions. Thus, to take an example from Ruth's Seventh Journey, when she goes right to the depths of Hell; why (one might ask) have legend and drama depicted the underworld traditionally in that particular 'negative green' light, and with fumes of sulphur? It was thought to be a conventional sign of the stage appearance of 'the evil one', but in fact it stems from a living experience; those who have been there know.

Turning to our European heritage in late medieval and early modern times, there are, of course, the great classical journeys of Dante, Bunyan, and Swedenborg. Much of their detail is inevitably coloured by the climates of thought, religion, morality and politics of the countries and historical periods concerned, but the basic archetypal landmarks—indeed many of the actual symbols—remain the same.

Coming to the present day, I am delighted to see the extent to which modern children's literature, with its many tales of 'cracks in time', mediates the fourth dimension to a generation which can respond immediately with unspoiled recognition. These books (to my mind) are of a quality far outranking that of most modern novels written for adults—always excepting Tolkien's *The Lord of the Rings* which is ageless in its appeal.

Many great poets have clearly 'been there'. Among modern poets I would single out T. S. Eliot, and here, perhaps, I might bring in a personal note. For many years beforehand, and also throughout all the work with Ruth, naturally I read everything I could, in as many idioms as possible, in order to try to understand the process. At the time of Ruth's journeys, however, I found Eliot particularly meaningful, and—strangely enough— of all his works *The Cocktail Party* gave me comfort; I think largely because of the contemporary setting where, instead of monastic or temple retreat, we have to function *in* the world and yet not be entirely *of* the world. Here was Celia, 'seeing through' ordinary life, yet by no means a 'psychological case'; and here were the three 'guardians', unknown as such in an outer-world context, living normal outer lives, yet, however uncertain consciously, knowing inwardly the responsibility of the part they had to play. And what else could they—or what else could I— do but recognize, accept, watch and pray?

Reilly
It is finished. You can come in now.
She will go far, that one.

* * * * *

Julia
Oh yes, she will go far. And we know where she is going.
But what do we know of the terrors of the journey?
You and I don't know the process by which the human is
Transhumanised : what do we know

Of the kind of suffering they must undergo
On the way of illumination?

*   *   *   *   *

Alex
The words for those who go upon a journey.

Reilly
Protector of travellers
Bless the road.

Alex
Watch over her in the desert.
Watch over her in the mountain.
Watch over her in the labyrinth.
Watch over her by the quicksand.

Julia
Protect her from the Voices
Protect her from the Visions
Protect her from the tumult
Protect her in the silence.

The Philosophical Approach: Subjective and Objective Reality

At this point, some 'well-earthed' readers may be thinking:
'Admittedly these phenomena have been widely recognized in
mythology and literature, but they are not *real*: they are pure
imagination—all in the mind.' (One reader went as far as to
suggest that the material might be 'a literary tour de force' of
my own—until he met Ruth!)

Here they must be challenged: What do you mean by
'reality'? Are there, perhaps, different *orders* of reality, or do
you recognize only the material order? And, (using the term
'mind' in its widest sense to include feeling and insight as well
as thought) how can we approach an understanding of any order
of reality *except* 'in the mind'?

First, do we accept that, in direct sense-experience, we know so-called 'outer reality' only in so far as it is perceived by our physical senses and then presented to our mental interpretation by the brain? But the brain, like a computer, has been 'programmed' through our education and especially our early conditioning to select and present impressions in certain conventionally accepted ways. If (as in some other cultures) our computers are programmed differently, they perceive, select and transmit in those specific ways, so that the mind comes to understand 'reality' in varied modes. Even in a common culture, the brains of no two individuals can be programmed completely identically, and therefore each is aware of a slightly different *effective* environment.

If this principle is accepted on the level of physical 'reality', can we then go one step further and agree that, as far as we can rely on our physical senses for the initial perceptions, our understanding is restricted to a three-dimensional 'world'? We are, then, limiting ourselves to a partial view only of total reality. (Research even in the material sciences shows that the physical world is far other than perceived by our physical senses.) But, if we develop our 'higher senses', and attempt to expand our awareness to receive and interpret—at least to some degree— what they tell us, we can then begin to comprehend the reality of further dimensions and modes of being. It is of very little use to try to research into multi-dimensional fields *in terms of* our limited three-dimensional tools and concepts. To do so is a semantic distortion—a restriction of the more complete meaning which can then be apprehended only partially, and this through the media of symbols and signs; much as in a photograph or representative drawing, the convention of perspective mediates the impression of three dimensions in terms of two; but the representation is not the reality.

Some initial methods of reaching the inner worlds are mentioned later in this chapter. But they are, of course, all techniques 'in the mind'. The question then arises as to the degree of the 'subjective' or 'objective' validity of the phenomena experienced, for naturally different individuals perceive different phenomena, although there is yet much in common.

First, what is understood by the terms? The term 'subjective'

I understand as denoting 'private worlds' in which images and appearances, although they may *seem* to be objective in that they appear 'out there' to the experiencing individual, are actually projections of his current state of being, or of that part of his forgotten past which is emerging for encounter. They are not usually experienced by others who inhabit either outer or inner 'worlds'. Thus in Ruth's Third Journey (Chapter Nine) Gildas explains that he and the baby do not experience the darkness and suffering which she does, although they are there, in the inner world, with her.

Such projections are necessary in order that they may be confronted, taken home, worked on, and eventually transmuted. The bulk of personality work, when carried out on inner levels, on the way of redemption, is of such a nature. To give these experiences the label of 'subjective', however, does not imply that they are not intensely real to the individual experiencing them. No one who has worked with people, as I have, through years of inner turmoil, suffering, and achievement, would ever doubt their *experiential* reality. (The process is described in detail in the Seventh Journey, Chapters Fourteen and Fifteen, so as to give the reader an impression of the way it feels.) In my definition, then, the experiences are those of *subjective reality in another dimension*— another order of being.

The term 'objective', as applied to experience, would appear to denote 'public worlds' in so far as most people share common perceptions and agree (in general) as to what these signify. This we find (with slight individual variations) in the three-dimensional outer world.

In inner-world journeys, however, although many of the landmarks are universal and archetypal, we are still a long way from finding such a degree of common experience. Far more development and research are necessary; my own knowledge is limited to a very few journeys. But one thing I have noticed, and I should be interested to know if other investigators find the same : the higher the travellers go in level of awareness, the more closely the quality of their experience matches. There are moments in Ruth's journeys, as for instance at Darwen Tower, at the ends of journeys, and particularly during initiations, when she touches that quality of knowledge of the higher nature of being which mystics have attempted to describe, and which—in the higher parts of ourselves—we all recognize and share, could we but register it.

An image common to many mystics is that of the conical Golden Mountain, or the Mountain of God. Those around the base of the mountain are aware of differences and of pairs of opposites: those at the North, looking at the peak, say that it lies to the South; those at the South are sure that it lies to the North; similarly with East and West; and all are right, at their level, and in that dimension. Each individual must travel, as it were, up his own valley to the peak, and he can only start from where he is. Each valley is a private world, and it does not do to try to follow the valley of another, for the individual is the transforming instrument of his own way, and therein he will find what he needs to find. However, as he climbs ever nearer to the summit—as he approaches cosmic consciousness—he finds the many paths inevitably converging; increasingly he shares with others common experiences, and particularly that awareness of the unity of all creation. At this level, the pairs of opposites subjective/objective, self/other, and many more, are transcended, for, as Traherne knew:

> 'All my mind was wholly everywhere,
> What'er it saw, 'twas ever wholly there;
> The sun ten thousand legions off, was nigh:
> > The utmost star,
> > Though seen from far,
> Was present in the apple of my eye.'

Perhaps it is only at this level that we can begin to *feel* the reality of what her Great Teacher told Ruth at the time of her dedication, after the Third Journey:

'Learn that all experience is given not for the individual alone but for humanity.'

For we realize—even if only in a flash beyond time—that if we are one with the whole field of being, every thought, feeling, action, achievement, and failure inevitably affects and modifies the whole energy-field—the pattern—on however microcosmic a scale. At the same time we know that the 'I' of itself can do very little in its own strength. As Gildas has so often said, its essential contribution is 'acceptance and commitment', in order that the higher self, which can see so much more extensively, can do the work, effecting the necessary changes at the right points in our time.

Yet while we are still limited to the 'I' consciousness as we toil up our valleys, this principle is beyond our full comprehension. At the outset of the Fourth Journey, Gildas told Ruth:

'All that you do in these journeys concerns not only you but others in a much wider field, in a way which you will one day understand, but for now you must trust me that this is so.'

Our part, then, is to keep climbing up our own Valley of the Shadow, redeeming the Shadow as we go, for this is the journey classically known as the way of purgation, between Earth (and—for some—Hell) and Paradise.

The Psychic Approach and Preparation for Mediumship

A commentary on Ruth's inner journeys in the light of the Ageless Wisdom, using the idiom of esoteric schools, is given in its proper time-context in Chapter Thirteen. It is, however, very important to realize that, as we raise the level of our awareness, so the further dimensions of being, with all the conditions that they imply (Hell, Purgatory, Paradise), form an increasingly conscious part of our daily life. What used to be thought of as 'happening after death' now, more and more frequently, can happen while we are still alive.

Thus, there are many accounts, in scripts purporting to come from those who have died, or from the teaching guides, describing the challenge, not long after death, when we must all 'look into the pool and love what we find'; we must work on the reflection of our immediately past life, finally understanding and accepting it all—the light and the dark—as aspects of total learning. This is usually described as a somewhat gruelling process which must be taken with courage, yet one which can also be shot through with unexpected joy. We have the help of our guides and teachers, and sometimes much of the work is done in relation to a group. In fact, some accounts sound similar to those of deeper psychotherapy.

Further, after the retrospect of this life ends (possibly back in the innocence of early childhood), a more extensive view may open up, at first in flashes or separate pieces like those of a jig-saw puzzle, each piece appropriate to the current learning situa-tion. For, we are told, learning continues, though perhaps in a different mode, throughout the planes; and there is much, often of darkness, to be transmuted and integrated, as the distilled strength and wisdom are gathered into the greater being for use in further lives. In the process, the deeper the darkness, the greater is the degree of redemption achieved, and therefore—eventually—the greater are the light and joy.

As the New Age comes into being, more and more individuals appear to be drawn to do this purgatorial work during their incarnate lives. I must stress, however, that not all of us are asked to endure what Ruth—and some other strong souls—have done and are doing. To each is given his own task, and no one is tried beyond his strength. Again, it is extremely unwise for the individual, or his adviser, to attempt to precipitate past-life work until there is clear readiness for it; the higher self knows the right moment in time if it is to be done at all. Further, the redemptive work may come in different forms and modes; to some it is presented in the pattern of outer or physical tests and trials; others work on it mainly inwardly, in partial or in full consciousness; most of us experience a degree of both aspects. Anyway, there are the comforting thoughts that the more we do now, the less we shall have to do after death, when it is often more difficult; and we are told that the eventual joy is equivalent to the suffering—indeed greater, 'pressed down and running over'. In fact, when we are committed in love and light, accept-ance and forgiveness, the learning process is hardly experienced as suffering at all, as Ruth found, to a large extent, in her Sixth Journey.

If this is happening to many ordinary people who do not have special extra-sensory abilities, how much more important is it, surely, for those 'sensitives' and mediums endowed with psychic gifts who work as channels between the dimensions!

But first: what is the place of the psychic faculties in the journey towards higher consciousness? Some spiritual and esoteric groups regard psychic powers as a dangerous side-track likely to fascinate for its own sake, to lend power and prestige to the little ego, and therefore to be rejected. But is not this the attitude of judging an ability by its abuse, just because in the past it has, indeed, been so greatly abused? As in the case of any human faculty, it is just when they are rejected or repressed that psychic functions tend to live an existence of their own, often on a low level of superstition or negative occultism, rendering health and wholeness of the personality impossible. I would therefore regard the psychic faculties as an integral part of human nature, and as potentially valuable aids in exploring higher worlds, *in so far as* they are accepted, educated, trained, and used with discrimination in the context of the healthy *spiritual* development both of the gifted individual and the group or groups with which he is associated.

In investigating the field of the psychic and of spiritualism, however, one finds many areas of conflict. For instance, there is the axis of difference between the 'scientific' and the 'mystical'. Some mediums show fear of the investigations and experimental outlook of psychical research and of parapsychology; they may therefore tend to identify with and defend their own powers, with resultant suspicion on both sides. But surely, if the experience is genuine, like gold it will come through the fire unharmed, as some of the greater mediums have shown us. Moreover, psychical research and parapsychology have much to learn from the quality of the higher teachings which come through. The modern trend, therefore, is to regard the whole issue on a higher level: to see the development of paranormal powers and of true mystical awareness as parts of the same process—a *linking* of the psychic and the spiritual for their mutual nourishment rather than their previous mutual distrust.

Then there is the unwillingness of many sensitives (again, not the great ones) to check the material that is perceived and transmitted through them *in terms of their own personality development.*

'I am concerned,' wrote a reader of the Gildas Teachings,

'about certain mediums who seem incapable of producing anything out of their own spiritual resources. Should they not give
up "channelling" and grow themselves? It seems as though the
pressures and preoccupations of mediumship have stultified their
own growth.'

Surely, the more the personality is 'grown', clarified, and
committed, the purer the channel? So much New Age teaching
lays emphasis on personal transformation before we are able even
to perceive, let alone transmit, the new truths. And long ago
Steiner established as a major principle that the only safe access
to the higher world is gained by striving for genuine knowledge
and assessment of one's own being.

This leads to the question of education for mediumship, both
in preparation beforehand and in 'in-service training'. Few would
question that the work of most sensitives is parallel to that of
other 'helping professions' such as social work, teaching, counselling and guidance—personnel work of all kinds, for they give
personal consultations at very intimate levels. Nowadays, in training for all these professions, there is increasing stress on personality work—sometimes with an individual counsellor or therapist,
but more often in therapeutic, 'encounter', or 'sensitivity' groups
of one kind or another, since the main instrument of the person
who works in human relationships *is* his personality. We hear
so much about 'cleansing the doors of perception', but little about
cleansing the rest of the psyche. Should not some form of personality-work be included in a training course so that the general
level of insight and self-understanding can be raised? (I am not
suggesting the crude type of group-work which might shatter a
delicately-balanced sensitive, but one in which spiritual exercises
such as meditation, prayer, and work with one's guides form
part of the study of self and relationship in action.) There are
then fewer dangers of ego-inflation or of contact with low-grade
'spirits' who otherwise might invade *via* the weak spots—the
less developed side of the personality which is common to all—
playing tricks, masquerading as famous beings, or even 'possess-
ing' the sensitive concerned.

In Ruth's case, as readers of *Gildas Communicates* will know,
after six of the journeys were over she took part with five others

of us in some psychological group-work of this kind; but the individual therapy with me, and the work with her own guide, came first. During most of the time, of course, we had no idea, apart from the obvious one of healing and growth, of any specific application; later however, looking back, we saw it as a most valuable basic *general* preparation for channelling Gildas' teaching and for any other work she may yet have to do. (I am not talking here of *specific* training for mediumship, which is outside my field. In fact, it was Gildas himself who gave Ruth courses of exercises in higher sense training and development, but these are beyond the scope of this book.)

The Approach from Psychotherapy

Even within that branch of applied psychology which gives a conceptual basis for mental healing, there are many schools of thought, often in conflict. Yet the more one works with different colleagues—Gestalt Therapists, Learning Theorists practising de-sensitization, Rogerian Counsellors, representatives of all the various Analytic Schools—the more one realizes that, although basic assumptions, levels and methods may vary, the processes and aims have much in common.

Even within the Analytic Schools—Orthodox Freudian, Neo-Freudian (several), Jungian, and many other offshoots—there are signs of rapprochement. As one analyst put it : 'I do not mind whether they speak of the Kleinian "Bad Breast" or the Jungian "Terrible Mother"; it is much the same.'

It is clear, therefore, that although the psychological aspect of inner journeys may be interpreted in various ways and at different depths, each interpretation is probably valid in its own idiom and at its own level. All approaches are useful provided that one is aware of the dangers of reducing a total experience to a partial explanation of it—trapped in a limited hypothetical construct by the separatist doctrine of 'nothing but'.

Thus, to take an example from Ruth's material : the constantly-recurring image of the primaeval swamp may be understood by Freudians as representing the (as yet) uncivilized 'Id' of the individual, its primitive instinctual forces manifesting in prehistoric saurian form. Or, by Jungians, it can be seen as a layer of the 'collective unconscious', particularly as the archetypal Earth-Mother in her swallowing, 'quicksand' aspect, sucking back to the undifferentiated collective the embryonic individual ego which must struggle out and on to the *terra firma* of conscious individuation. Yet again, by some spiritual psychotherapists it can be perceived as the *prima materia* needing redemption through the instrument of the incarnating spirit—the Christ principle.

To take another example: 'the angel'—Gildas himself—changing his relationship to Ruth as was appropriate throughout different stages of his guiding and teaching. Is he, as Freudians might suggest, especially in the early stages, the 'Oedipal' image of the Father-figure—an idealized projection? Is he (in Jungian terms) playing various 'Animus' roles or the part of the 'Old Wise Man'? To quote again from *Gildas Communicates,* this was the very first thing I asked him when, in 1962, he started answering my questions.

'Who are you,' I asked, 'from your point of view? Spiritualists would call you a "guide", Jungian psychologists the "Animus" part of Ruth's psyche. How do you see yourself?' He replied:

'Perhaps the spiritualists are more correct than the Jungians, for I am indeed a separate entity in many respects. I do not exist solely as a part of Ruth. We are linked from ages past, the perfect partners, able to live apart yet incomplete without each other. We have lived lives apart, we have also incarnated together, and now I have achieved a state where I can live separately and yet within Ruth. She sees me as a separate being, yet I never really leave her, for our spirits are so intermingled in the web of time and the pattern of life that we are never really apart. I leave her and come and go in my "bodily" aspect, yet remaining ever within her and she within me in another aspect —that of completeness.'

He then went on to what is, perhaps, his central teaching:

'A truth, like a jewel, has many facets. These theories which are held by different schools and different people are often part of the truth, yet not the whole of it, and, like a jewel, the true value and beauty is only seen when one holds the complete thing. Oh that men would achieve the humility to see this—how much valuable energy would be saved for other things! Therefore to some extent our relationship can be understood in any of these ways, but only when an attempt is made to accept the universal truth are you near the actuality.'

Much earlier than this, in 1959, he had told Ruth, 'I don't want you to get the idea that I am *part* of psychotherapy—that I am particularly linked with this process of analysis. In some ways, of course, I am, but I have a life outside the analytical experience too.' (See p. 84.)

Nevertheless, after the Sixth Journey was over, Gildas did ask us to make a study of all the journeys together, so as to understand them as a whole and in all possible aspects. The psychic/spiritual commentary, which I wrote for Ruth as a basis for discussion, is given in Chapter Thirteen, but we also carried out a thoroughly theoretical review of the psychological aspects. During the actual process of work, as psychotherapists will readily understand, theory and jargon had been kept to a minimum, but later (1964 onwards) Ruth studied the theoretical notes of my course on training for psychological counselling, and also the specific, detailed commentaries which I wrote on her journeys. In subsequent discussion we attempted some intellectual consolidation on many levels. Obviously the material is too private and personal to be described here, but the following brief outline may give a rough guide.

Following Freud, Klein, and (largely) Fairbairn, we traced the pattern as a reductive one, going backwards from the adolescent problems of the First Journey through childhood to infancy, through all the classical phases to the redemption of Winnicott's 'True Self', or Fairbairn's 'regressed ego'.

In Jungian terminology, we saw the confrontation with the major archetypes on the path of individuation : the Persona; the Shadow; the Animus; and particularly the Great Mother in her many-faced aspects. Throughout the journeys the Self appears in many images—perhaps most frequently as the Rock; and the Transforming Symbol of wholeness—the Jewel found in the First Journey—is used throughout. Gildas has commented :

'If I am enabled to awaken your sensitivities to the ultimate oneness of all theories around a subject—to begin to show you

31

new vistas for creative thought, then much of my purpose shall have been accomplished.'

There was one respect in which psychotherapy with Ruth was (almost) unique, at least to me; it is very rarely that one can share the work with an inner Guide; but this experience was a great joy, and an immense relief when areas as far as I knew yet uncharted were encountered. Gildas and I worked together with Ruth in complementary fashion; he on the inner and I on the outer. Several times in the scripts it will be noted that he referred Ruth to me where psychological personality-work, or the feminine approach, was needed. On my part, when we became 'stuck' in trying to understand an image—or pure imageless darkness and suffering—I would often ask Ruth, 'What does Gildas suggest?' She would 'tune in' for a moment and report. He *never* did the work for her; often indeed he refused to answer, or merely said, 'Live it through' or 'Go on working at it', or some such phrase; but sometimes he directed our attention to that aspect of an image which neither she nor I had thought of, and this would help to release the block. This close co-operation between the person undergoing therapy, her inner guide, and her outer therapist is a delightful partnership, and one which may well develop more widely in the future.

At one stage, Gildas gave me a valid criticism, pin-pointing my weak spot as a therapist (see p. 85), when he felt that I was being over-sensitive and afraid to hurt Ruth. (Though regretting the necessity, he himself had no qualms about scourging her when necessary in the early stages—a fact which may possibly shock some readers.) What I had to learn to accept—without guilt and without trying to alleviate it—was the degree, depth and prolonged extent of Ruth's suffering, and perhaps some readers may feel with me in this as they read the agony of most of the journeys. Once I had fully accepted that she had chosen, in her higher self, to suffer like this, things went better.

What worried me—and I think may well concern and even horrify most qualified psychotherapists—was the very limited amount of time we had in which to work together. In view of the depth of the experiences, some would consider that ideally Ruth should have had intensive psychotherapy, even several times

32

a week over several years. Unfortunately, this was completely impracticable, but, for interest, here are the figures :

As a student in 1957/58 (the First Journey) she had twenty-one interviews. As a teacher, working in the area, she had fourteen interviews in 1958/59, seventeen in 1959/60, and twenty-two in 1960/61—a total of seventy-four interviews only, spread over the first four years, and taking us up to the end of the Third Journey.

In 1961 she married and went to live at a considerable distance from my home. From then on, our relationship changed to that of friends and colleagues, but meetings were sporadic. We usually managed one intensive week, at her home, once a year. Also some personal work was done (usually a daily hour over early-morning tea) during the annual few days spent with our inner group, but that was all. Most communication had to be by letter, and, as the demand for 'The Gildas Teachings' grew rapidly from 1962 onwards, the pressure became increasingly greater, taking up most of the time when we could meet. Therefore, almost all the later work, from the Fourth Journey onwards, Ruth did on her own, particularly in the Fifth Journey when she was allowed to tell no one until it was over. Doubtless all this was part of the essential pattern. In the Seventh Journey (Chapters Fourteen and Fifteen) is a detailed description of the way we had to work! We did our best; no one can do more.

Methods of Reaching the Inner World

Individuals approach the inner life in different ways : natural introverts usually more directly, extraverts more through reflection from outer actions, objects, and happenings. Again, the relative emphasis may change according to the phase of life. To take my own case : during many years of psychological analysis and also of work in a spiritual school—and particularly during the change of life—I had considerable direct experience (though not comparable to Ruth's); now, in the relatively extravert phase of the later fifties and sixties, inner guidance is mediated largely through intuitive 'hunches' concerning practical work to be done in daily living and relationships.

Even in the case of those open to direct inner experience, the impact of the numinous is generally mediated through symbols which form relatively concrete images, however deeply felt : the cross, the tree, the well. In Ruth's case, there are 'tangible' symbols of swords, monsters, bones, and mud. The 'left hand path' is not known *first* in its classical allegorical significance as the evil way, but is literally seen as an actual path on the left side of the Way. The 'transforming symbol' is not perceived immediately as the idea—the principle of perfect wholeness which includes all things—but appears first as a tangible, perfectly-formed jewel of myriad facets. Much of the work to be done after the experience lies in the full realization—in every aspect of one's being—of what these symbols mean.

However, with these qualifications, here is a list of some of the methods of access which can be used :

The dream, which is usually completely cut off from waking life. It can be understood on levels ranging from true dreams and memories of events in the sleep state, through the more frequent symbolic dreams (the 'happy hunting ground' of psycho-therapists) to the relatively insignificant reproductions of daily happenings or of physical states.

Images on the edge of sleep (the so-called hypnogogic and hypnopompic images).

Spontaneous visions, auditory or any other form of extra-sensory perception.

Spontaneous day dreams or persistent phantasies (again, at varying levels).

Willed 'reverie', Jungian 'active imagination', or Progoff's 'twilight imaging'.

Meditation (of various kinds and depths).

Actual fully-conscious inner living, by those who can 'shift level', when the inner world can appear to be as real as the outer, if not more so.

Some people can gain access to their greater psyche more readily when it is reflected back to them from their hands, voices, bodies, and behaviour generally. Hence the value of free writing, painting, modelling, drama, and dance. (Possibly the use of the pendulum might come in this category.)

To others again the journey is an altogether outer-world affair of happenings, of coping with relationships and with 'solid reality'.

Whichever ways are found most congenial, the outer does mirror the inner, and *vice versa*. As Ruth knew in the end, all modes of experience are one.

In her journeys, Ruth used all these techniques. When there was resistance in confronting some aspect of her psyche, she often used free writing, or listened to what her body was trying to tell her in its language of cold, heaviness, tension, or pain. Painting was useful in order to express a burst of fury when it came welling up at inconvenient times. I well remember one summer evening when she had difficulty in finding and accepting a particularly elusive part of her psyche which was just emerging into consciousness. 'I could dance it,' she said, 'but you must dance too.' So we went out on to the lawn where her spontaneous movement led to discovery and recognition. Following my own intuition, I found myself simply moving in a clockwise circle around the edge of my oblong lawn; later I realized that I had been dancing the containing *temenos*. But Ruth's main ways were dreams, visions, active imagination (or, to use Gildas' happy term, 'creative imagination'), meditation, and above all direct, conscious experience.

Ruth grew up in the framework of an orthodox Christian belief. Although in this context she had experience of prayer and meditation, there had been nothing, either at home or at school, to introduce her to esoteric and psychic science, so that when—at nineteen—her inner life began to take the form of these journeys, she had a severe problem of sorting out her religious beliefs (see pp. 59 and 133–4).

At first the experiences came in dreams which we interpreted at the usual psychological level; but soon we found a deeper level where the figure of 'the angel' (Gildas) spoke for himself. Ruth then found herself listening to a revelation of truth in a new and living way—living because his teaching was invariably applied to each phase of her progressive experience. Thus, when Gildas first began to answer my questions, after the Third Journey in 1962, I asked him for some teaching on cosmology. He replied, 'Ruth learns through experience, and each

35

experience makes her ready for a little more. When Ruth herself is ready I shall be glad to give this teaching, it is much needed; but I cannot give teaching through Ruth about things which she cannot, as yet, know and accept with every part of her.' (During the succeeding twelve years, however, very much more has been given.)

Ruth has said, 'The help came mainly through dreams at first . . . then Gildas came into the first ones. When I found that this was someone I could contact by writing (he was saying things that didn't seem to be coming from me) then I began to see him and know him.' His words would come into her mind like dictation, and she would write them down. She always worked in full consciousness, never in the trance state.

To return to the journeys : as she went deeply into them, the inner life would continue consciously during the day as well as in sleep-dreams. She never lost contact with outer reality, keeping her balance, and carrying on with her professional and home life even through the worst of the experiences, although at times this was very difficult. She describes her position very clearly during the Fourth Journey (p. 148).

When working deliberately on the crucial transformation of symbols, such as the Monsters and the Octopus (Chapter Four) she would often use 'creative imagination' which needs immense concentration of positive energy and light to effect the change. Those readers who are interested in methods will recognize the different techniques which we have noted, as far as possible, throughout the work.

Patterns in Journeys

What is found by means of these techniques has an immense range in quality from the 'bad trip' of the drug-taker to the inexpressible glories revealed to disciplined mystics. It varies also in degree of conscious awareness; many of us may be living and experiencing intensely on other levels, especially during sleep, but in a mode which cannot register on the slowly-vibrating physical brain except, perhaps, in the merest flash of a 'true dream' on waking. One man told me that, in those moments when just falling asleep or waking up, he was aware of an intensely greater speed of thought and being—a higher frequency as it were—but could capture no more, though he knew he had been both hearing and saying far more meaningful things than he could do in ordinary life (he is a brilliant university lecturer). Some, with more continuous awareness, yet who cannot be said to be on 'the journey proper', have inner landscapes which they can always contact in twilight reverie; so real are these to a few that they have mapped them. Although always there, and accessible, they tend to change character in relation to the phase of development of the individual concerned and the outer lessons to be learned, but they cannot be altered by conscious will. These landscapes may be inhabited by animals and other people; events may take place which are beyond conscious manipulation; some people feel themselves to be living in the scenes, others—like observers—watch the figures—including themselves—acting upon an inner screen. All these dramatic forms are invaluable grist to the mill of self-knowledge.

Coming to the 'journey proper': in Chapter Thirteen, which was written in 1964, I have referred briefly to the classical stages. With regard to the initial 'Call', however, since then I have met a young man who *felt* (though did not *see*) the goal of the journey right from the outset. He did not, like some, attempt to stay there; he knew he had to find and live it through in this life. He wrote :

'To begin a journey needs first of all a sense of purpose.

'One afternoon, whilst listening to Beethoven's Seventh Symphony on a purely intellectual level, I recognized that for this music to have relevance for others in a different time and mode of life, it must mean that there were certain life experiences common to all. At this point I became aware of a sense of timelessness; then this concept, which I had logically deduced, became a force which flooded the room. The description defies my literary powers : it was as if time stood still and revealed to me an essence and a meaning. I felt that now I saw the meaning of Eternity—a new dimension of life; that there was a spiritual force above but within man's existence in the physical world. The universe became a living organism of process with purpose. This aspect was revealed to me as a force of goodness and love, and I became enveloped in these forces; they did, however, originate in part from within me. This fusion made me at one with the universe, its history and meaning. The secret of life became mine. I was filled with a marvellous joy at the revelation of the true role of man.

'As the sensation receded, I knew that what I had experienced was the answer and the goal of life: to establish this harmony was both the meaning and omega of man's earthly life. My life became a journey to fulfil my essence, of a union with the universe and union with the forces of goodness and love. If I knew the destiny and purpose, I did not as yet know the way.'

And then, unknowing, he set out upon his journey.

Where does the journey go? Classically into the inner world and out again: 'The Withdrawal and Return'; 'There and Back Again'; down to the depths of the psyche (or to the centre of the earth, or to the bottom of the sea, as some have it) and up again —but always up again by a new way. And the inner geography, although differing in detail for each individual, has a universal pattern common to all.

The common pattern is recognized first in the basic symbols and archetypes: the snake, cave, fountain, jewel, desert, golden flower—staff—orb——and many many more. I have not dared to attempt an analysis of symbols; there are encyclopaedias of mythology and symbolism, and those interested will find that a whole treatise could be written on each one. (This is a fascinating topic for research; why, for example, I asked myself as I typed the First Journey for this book, do lions and lizards—incongruous pair—challenge Ruth at the outset of her journeys? And into my mind came a phrase from Omar Khayyam—a fragment of ancient wisdom?—'They say the Lion and the Lizard keep/ The Courts...') Yet I must stress that these are *symbols*, not mere *signs*. A symbol is a living experience, deeply felt, mediating the numinous, and pregnant with power. Further, in the case of any valid symbol, it may be meaningful at many different levels, all of them true: that of the personal conscious; the personal unconscious; the human collective; the basic biological; the cosmic. Again, the work to be done with these images is redemptive; the lower forms present themselves for transmutation; (as my analyst used to say, they *want* to be changed, to evolve.) Whether they evolve by death and re-birth in another form, or by loving-into-change, depends on the nature of the creature and what it symbolizes. Thus Ruth was told to kill the large Monsters of Pride but to care for the young one who might then change into that independent, self-respecting, domestic animal, the cat. Some, like the revolting sub-human child of the Fifth Journey, must be raised in 'frequency of vibration' by acceptance and love, 'stepped up' so that they become warm, light and beautiful instead of cold, dark and ugly. This is the Frog Prince myth which all children instinctively recognize as true.

Some of the major archetypes need a whole series of trans-formations, each one of a different aspect. An example of a series from Ruth's work is that of the Great Mother who appears at all levels and is many-faced. Apart from the more conscious levels, and the swamp already mentioned, we meet her first in one of her classical negative forms as the possessive Octopus. After killing this image, and gaining from it the Golden Staff, Ruth has to put in considerable long and hard work constellating the positive mother image by being herself a 'good mother' to the children and Astra. Only then, for the first time, is she given a vision of the Divine Mother who appears—interestingly enough —again in classical form : literally *anadyomene*, i.e. 'rising from the waters' (p. 96). I understand that Ruth had no conscious knowledge at the time of the tradition of the birth of Aphrodite.

But another aspect must be redeemed. At the end of the Third Journey Ruth speaks of the transformation of the Witch figure 'from all her horror into a beautiful statue of purest white, with flowing lines which seemed to link earth with heaven'. (We have no previous mention in the scripts of the Witch image, but in her private psychotherapy this had appeared, and temporarily Ruth had seen me in this capacity!) Later on, when she is ready and stronger, a still deeper layer must be confronted, at the very bottom of the sea (the unconscious?) in the appalling form of the Green Sea Witch of the Fourth Journey. After this, in the Fifth, she has herself to be mother and guide to a soul on the karmic level. Then, in the Sixth, comes the final painless re-birth from the womb of the Great Mother in her positive aspect of the gentle, warm, soft, moist, fruitful Earth itself. (Three months afterwards, in October 1964, Ruth's daughter was born in the outer world, so the timing was perfect.) Four years later, we find the Divine Mother appearing in a completely accepting and helpful way at two critical stages of the Seventh Journey: in the Christian context of the Church of St. Mary the Virgin, and— right at the very end—waiting for Ruth outside the gates of Hell.

Some readers may be surprised at the birth of Astra and Michael, Ruth's 'inner children'. Questioned by me about this, Gildas said in 1962, 'I will assure you that Ruth's experiences of childbirth are very real, and she will be able to give you even more assurance of this when she has borne a physical child; she will know the pattern in a sure and beautiful way and will be able to experience to the full the wonder of bearing a new life. Because she has experienced it before, she will be relaxed and fearless.' As in the case of motherhood and childbirth, it is significant that many other major experiences and relationships of earthly life are practised, as it were, on the inner before manifesting on the outer. Thus Gildas changes his role ('I am not the stern parent'—p. 102) to that of lover and husband *before* Ruth is married in the outer world, and there are many more examples. Did we but know it, perhaps we could learn a good deal from the higher worlds before we live it through in the here-and-now.

In all this work, there is a very close relationship between inner and outer. Just for some light relief and fun, we have included a bit of telepathic 'play' in the Interlude (Chapter Eight) when I sent a present of a Teddy Bear to Astra. As a child I had a white bear which I called 'Polar Bear'. Since most Teddies are brown I thought this might be an unusual thought-form to send, and to a large extent it worked. This opens quite a field of possibilities in sending presents to children on the Astral planes!

Writing of Astra introduces the supremely important matter of different dimensions of time. In our time, Astra was born in August 1959. But when Gildas brings her to Ruth after the end of the Second Journey in August 1960, instead of being a baby of one year old, she is a child of about five. Gildas explains:

'Our time is not as yours ... You can tell from the change in

Astra that your struggle has lasted a far longer time in the inner world than in the outer, and you have often been aware during this time that a particular task or battle has seemed to cover months in the inner world— yet in the outer only a comparatively short time has passed.' Other examples will be found of this difference in experience of *duration*.

Yet the actual *timing* of happenings, from the inner into our calendar-time, is remarkably exact. In Chapter Four, when Ruth is ready to face the Monsters, Gildas says, 'That time is here now. You have scratched the surface of some problems before, but now is the time to tackle them on a deeper and more permanent level, and remember that the inner forces are never wrong in their timing and estimations.'

One pattern (which I only noticed when re-editing the records for this book) is the number of occasions when major transformations or special ceremonies occur on a Sunday. We have already noted in *Gildas Communicates* that the battle with the elemental and the liberation of the flame in Northumberland came to a climax in the early hours of a Sunday morning. And now, in Ruth's journeys, I find:

Her marriage to Gildas was on Easter Sunday, 1960.

The Second Journey came to a climax and ended on Sunday, August 21st 1960.

Michael Arthor was conceived on Sunday, September 4th 1960, and was born on Sunday, May 14th 1961.

The Third Journey came to a climax and ended on Sunday, July 23rd 1961.

Ruth's dedication and initiation took place on Sunday, September 3rd 1961.

Lastly, the Seventh Journey ended in a final victory on Sunday, August 18th 1968.

For all I know, this pattern may also have applied to the First Fourth, Fifth and Sixth Journeys, but as they were not kept in diary form, we have no check. Whether this emphasis has any special significance as a day when the Christ power is especially strong, or whether it is simply that this is a non-working day with more time to give to inner work, I do not know; I simply record it.

Another interesting aspect of timing is the resonance between individual and cosmic patterns. The most striking example from Ruth's work is the culmination of the Seventh Journey in August 1968, when she gave birth to the dark jewel; and finally, winning freedom from the dark powers, she brought light into the heart of Hell. Is it significant that Gildas warned us that there was a very fine balance between light and dark in the world, and that the scales did tip to victory between July and September of that year? (*Gildas Communicates*, p. 102.) Some might see Gildas' comment as stemming from Ruth's subjective state; others might understand Ruth's experience as her personal contribution towards the greater victory, or as a reflection in her own life of the cosmic event. Going beyond arguments based on mere linear causality, however, it is undeniable that there is a synchronicity; there is a sharing by the individual in 'the togetherness of things'.

A third aspect of timing, especially applicable when there is a series of journeys, is that of progressive repetition. Readers of the original scripts have commented on the repetition, and in editing we have tried to eliminate all that is unnecessary; but it would falsify the process to cut it out where meaningful. Anyone who has experienced this type of inner searching, whether at psychological, esoteric, or spiritual levels, knows that all sound growth must be slow, and that the Way is circular—or rather spiral : the same ground must be covered again and again, but each time more deeply and with greater knowledge and confidence. It is essential to accept this pattern, and not to try to hurry the process, for in true education, 'readiness is all'. In this way, we work inwards, spirally, from outer social relationships and problems of the present, through childhood patterns in this life, back to karmic debts from past lives and so to archetypal levels. Some examples from Ruth's material may serve to illustrate these principles.

The fire-test appears many times. At the start of the First Journey, she is afraid, and so gets badly burned. When it recurs in the Second, she has no fear so takes it easily. Not until the Third, however, when completely consumed (the most painful part of the journeys) in the crater of the Fire-Mountain, can she 'walk forth, conqueror of the fire.' By the time she reaches the

Fifth, she is able to assure the child that there is no need to fear the fire; and in the Sixth, out of the heart of the white-hot fire she plucks the coal which becomes the sphere of pure gold.

The same developments may be seen in respect of the other elements : earth, water and air, as well as in constantly recurring images such as water-weeds, thorns, blood, bones, snakes, and many more. Often a landscape or symbol receives a mere mention in one journey, is dealt with more fully in another, resolved in a third, and finally used to help others in a fourth.

The karmic content emerges into consciousness only very gradually. At first (Chapter Three) a personal problem is resolved at a purely unconscious level during a moment of higher awareness on the tower above Darwen. The first flash-back to an obviously historical period occurs (with no explanation) in the Second Journey when children are killed and their blood runs in the streets. There is more than a hint of the attraction of Black Magic on the left-hand path in the Third Journey, but not until the Fourth does Gildas discuss karma overtly in relation to other lives; and then comes the crucial battle with these evil forces during Ruth's enclosure in the sarcophagus. The Fifth Journey is known from the beginning to be a karmic task. After the Sixth, Gildas tells Ruth much more about her past lives and activities between lives.

The set of Six Journeys, symbolized by the Hexagon, was evidently planned by Ruth's higher self before incarnation, though subject, of course, to her free will as explained by Gildas (p. 128). But the Seventh was to a greater degree a voluntary offering, and with a content which was far more trans-personal. For example, the prehistoric lizard-like saurians have occurred in one form or another throughout the whole work, different aspects being tackled each time. But the immense 'saurian tail', which is embedded deeply in the earth, is a well-known Jungian symbol of the most inaccessible part of the collective 'Shadow', and it is not until the Seventh Journey that Ruth penetrates right to the very tip of the tail, re-activating the 'inert gold' which she finds there. (I have not read of similar accounts of reaching the end of the tail, and should be interested to hear of any.) And it is on this Seventh Journey that Ruth plumbs the uttermost depths of her dark work in Atlantis, describing also its karmic retribution in Egypt; in redeeming all this she clears the karma right back to the primal 'golden seed'. There is infinitely more to explore and to attempt to understand, but perhaps these very brief pointers may serve to prepare the way.

Here, then, are some of the varying patterns which I have found to occur during journeys. Finally, what of the return?

Since journeys take place in another dimension of time, they do not 'end' in our sequent time. The return may at first feel like coming up from the depths, or down from the heights, but then *out*—as it were at a tangent—into the three-dimensional world. We emerge from the primal, timeless realm of archetypal energies to their application in daily living. We come back to 'concrete reality'—to the kitchen sink—much as Sam, at the end of *The Lord of the Rings* saga, comes home and says simply, 'Well, I'm back.'

So, to come back now into our time, and the beginning of the story: I was working as a psychological counsellor and psychotherapist for student teachers when I first met Ruth. She was nineteen, and at the beginning of her second year of the two-year course for infant teaching. During her adolescence she had been prevented from much studying because she had suffered—and was still suffering—from eye trouble; indeed she had been told by an oculist that she might go blind. Naturally, she was somewhat depressed about this situation, and came to consult me. This was the way in to the journeys.

CHAPTER 2

The Dream and the First Journey

November 1957 to May 1958

By Mary

Ruth was referred to me in late October, but counselling soon deepened into psychotherapy and later went far beyond. From the third interview she began to bring material which she called 'The Dream' though to her it felt like real, if subjective, experience.

She was walking, very frightened, alone along a narrow ridge. All was dark. When she went to the end of the ridge, it just stopped; below was nothing but darkness. Yet, in active imagination during an interview, she trusted the air, jumped off, and was wafted down gently into a wood, beautiful with green moss and sunlight. There she remained, happy to be alone.

Frequent inner images showed her perched on cliffs, mountains and tree-tops where she felt safe from the world below; in one she could see herself on the edge of a very high sea-cliff, higher than all the others. She fell over into the sea and her dead body was washed up on a rock. The defences at this early stage were very strong, and to be respected. Yet some dreams indicated the way to be taken :

She was in the park where she had played as a child. Children were sailing boats like boxes on the water. Then Ruth, in her boat, went down a river which divided into three. Following the left-hand stream, she came to a wood which was swampy and filled with prehistoric reptiles. The valley narrowed to a gorge but she could see light ahead.

Later, feeling unhappy and confused, she found herself walking through a wood (this time not swampy) where she lay down to sleep. On awakening she saw an enormous snake, fawn-coloured, like a python. It fought her and she fought back. Finally she gave in, accepting the snake. It then crawled along beside her and they came out of the wood together, friends, into the light. Continuing this dream/experience in active imagination, Ruth, with the snake, came to a river. The snake made a bridge over the river so that Ruth was able to walk across. Then they both sat down on the other side.

In working on this symbolism, Ruth associated the snake with that hidden part of herself which wanted to live, and which she had not previously let out. In Jungian terminology, this was the first aspect of the 'Shadow' to be encountered and integrated in friendship, thus freeing a great deal of previously repressed psychic energy for future use. It is interesting that the friendly snake was to lead eventually to the meeting with 'the angel'. For a while, however, there came a swing back to the defences—understandable in view of final teaching practice which was presenting a severe test in the outer world. Twelve times, with no modifications, was this dream repeated :

'It's an oblong garden with a kind of tree-top walk around it and the most beautiful flowers in it, and I'm miles up above them, going round the tree-top walk. Then you are in the garden and you tell me to come down. And I won't for a long time. When I do, you tell me to pick the flowers, but I don't, so you go away, you are quite cross about it. I curl up in a corner. Then a terrific wind comes and sweeps everything away—all the flowers have gone, all the tree-top walk, everything. It pours with rain and I half get up and see there's only one thing left in the garden, and that is this bench. I get on it and see there are all these lions around and I'm terrified. So I climb up on to the back of the bench and some kind of bird-like creature comes and carries me with its beak by the scruff of my neck up and up—we seem to go up for hours—and then it drops me on a precipice. I'm almost falling off but I manage to climb on to a ledge and then I crawl into a great black cave. I just feel miserable.' Ruth said that she liked being up in her tree-top walk, but the cave, to her, meant death. After working on this dream, she had another, once only, in which the snake appeared as her companion:

'I was still in the cave, facing inwards. There was something pushing from behind, making me go on, and I didn't want to, so I tried to cling on to the pillars like stalactites and stalagmites, but the force was too strong, so I had to go on. I was afraid to look round and see what it was. Then I came to a patch of briars, brambles and all kinds of prickly things, which I had to scramble through. On the other side there was a patch of nasty mud, oozy slimy stuff, and I had to wade through this almost up to my neck. But on the other side of the mud, the cave got lighter, and I met the snake. I had a friendly feeling; I was glad to see it. Then we could see the end of the cave—the light. (The cave went right through the mountain.) Dawn light. We came out on a ledge, very high up with steps going down into a sunlit dell. I was happy when I got there. I sang and laughed and danced. The snake just sat there and watched.'

And now, for the first time, we find the figure later to be known as Gildas. Every night for about a week:

'I was in a swimming pool. It was nice and I was enjoying myself. Then quite suddenly the swimming pool changed and was a horrid dark forest with mud and prehistoric animals—great lizards. I went on swimming through all this mud. I was terrified. Eventually I came to the end of the forest where I could see out. There was a white mountain with a spring gushing out. On either side of the spring there was a ledge. On one ledge sat the snake with a white robe beside him; on the other was a kind of angel all in white. I wanted to get out and wash in the spring and put on the white robe and be with the snake. I made a superhuman effort to get out of the swamp. But the lizards rose up and pushed me down into the mud, and I just went on sinking. Then I woke up.'

Mid-February coincided with the most critical time in the outer world: the final teaching practice assessment. Apart from continuous dreams of lizards, two nights before the ordeal Ruth had an even more alarming experience. She was on top of a mountain and a great boulder was falling on her. She avoided it but fell into a chasm at the bottom of which was a river which swept her away.

This was the turning point as far as the practical aspect of psychotherapy was concerned—*at the level possible at this time.*

In March Ruth was still struggling through the swamp with the great lizards all around. They still tried to push her down, but now she was stronger than they. She climbed out of the mud, walked through the forest and came to the white mountain. There she bathed in the spring and put on the white garment. Then she had to go with the angel along a ledge that ran round the mountain to the right. (The angel was on the right, the snake on the left, of the spring.) She was upset about this because she didn't want to leave the snake, whom she trusted. He also wanted to come with her, but he said he must wait until she came back. So she went with the angel round the ledge until she came to a corner. Then she was so frightened that she woke up in a panic—terrified that if she went round the corner she would never come back. She did not yet trust the angel and was now not even sure whether she could trust the snake.

Later the dream changed, though the new variant was still repeated nightly. She had gone round the corner of the ledge, following the angel. They went into a cave in which was a great fire. The angel said they must walk through the fire, and that if she were not frightened she would be unhurt. The angel went first to show how easy it was. But then she took the opportunity to go back to where the snake had been, only to find that the ledge was empty and everything was dark. So there was nothing for it but to return and go through the fire which she did in great fear, with the result that she was dreadfully scorched and her white robe burned right up. On the other side of the fire they came to a desert which must be crossed.

The next—and deepest—part of the whole experience was sent to me in letters during the Easter vacation:

'The dream which I was telling you about is most interesting; it just seems to go on and on, and although I have woken up crying once or twice, I'm not really frightened of it any more—

just interested. It's like a kind of serial story—sometimes an episode is repeated more than once, sometimes not—but almost every night I dream about something in the sequence. Let me tell you about it.

'After I'd recovered a little from walking through the fire, the angel led the way into the desert. It was hot—unbearably so, every muscle and every bone in my body ached, sweat poured off me, and the sand seemed to irritate my skin at every step. (Writing this down is like reliving it—in fact the experience is coming to me so vividly again—it's almost frightening.) I desperately wanted water, and kept asking for it, but always it was refused by the angel. After what seemed hours, we came to some rocks, which the angel would have passed by, but I had a sudden conviction that the snake might be hidden there and that if only I could find him all trial and tribulation would be over. Despite the angel's assertions that my search would be in vain, I ran to the rocks, and spent vital energy in a desperate hysterical search for something which I never found. In the end I went almost mad with the agony of it all, and the angel looked on sorrowfully as I banged my head against the rocks. Soon I was completely exhausted and burst into uncontrollable sobs. (I woke up crying.)

'The next night the dream continued. We had left the rocks far behind—the angel told me that I had slept for a while—and I certainly felt refreshed. The desert stretched on and on. Several times I thought we had reached the end but still it stretched before us—a desolate, barren waste. When I felt I could not move a step further, a great wind came, we were blinded with sand, but after a while there was a complete calm—the desert had been blown away, and all that remained was smooth white rock. In front of us was a sheer face of white rock, towering, it seemed, up and up, without end. The angel said we must pass through the rock, and if only I would believe the feat possible, it was easy to walk straight through the rock face. Unfortunately I did not believe this, and I wished to scale the rock and pass over the top. But the face was smooth, almost like glass, and with the top nowhere in sight it was an impossible task. I tried to find a way round the rock—but the face stretched endlessly—

I could find no end. Always I returned to where the angel waited patiently. (Here I woke up and this episode of the dream was repeated several times.)

'When the dream moved on a stage, I was still desperately looking for a way round or over the rock, without going through —but now it began to rain; the rock beneath us began to turn to swamp, and the lizards came back, threatening to push me deep down into the mud. Suddenly I found the determination to will the rock to open. I hurled myself against it—and to my great surprise passed through very easily. (This episode was also repeated two or three times.)

'The last part of this dream, so far, I dreamed last night—it is very short. The angel and I were in a dim cave lit with a green light. In the middle of the cave was a seething, white, boiling mass, all bubbles and slime, and utterly repulsive. I turned away in horror. Without the angel's telling me, I knew that I must find the courage to wade or swim through the mass—but I remembered the fire, and knew my courage must be absolute, or I should be scathed by this horror as I had been by the fire.'

(Later)

'Here is a copy of my record of the "inner journey". I assure you it is an exact copy of the original, though I was tempted to leave bits out! . . . The trouble is it's not all "sleep dream": half of it is "day dream", and I hardly know which is which. There came a time—which has now passed a little—when I seemed to be perpetually living in a dream-world; all concentration left me; all I could do was dream (and curse because unfortunately my work has suffered!) But I'm sure you'll agree with me when you read it all, that this inner journey is very wonderful. It is no longer terrifying, and I only hope that you are right when you say you think it will work out in the outer planes. I'm sure I can bear the suffering if the joy is comparable to that of the dream!

'Before me was a pool of boiling white stuff, utterly repulsive. I knew without the angel's telling me that I must walk through it. Suddenly, all fear left me, I felt a new confidence surging within me. I passed through the repulsive mass and my confidence was such that I remained untouched by it. The angel, somehow or other, had reached the other side before me, and now, for the first time on the journey, he smiled at me. Suddenly I relaxed—it was as if something within me had broken loose— I was happy—at last. Then the angel spoke, gently and kindly. "This is your first real success, but the suffering is not over yet— you still have much to learn, and some of the journey will be just as terrifying as before, but remember this moment of happiness, keep a firm hold on your new confidence, and soon you will find joy, greater than you can possibly imagine. You will face life with the deepest trust; you will gain a sense of fulfilment and contentment."

'As he was speaking, we had moved into another cave—very much like the first one of the journey—filled with fire, but how different this time was my reaction! I walked calmly and confidently through the flames and came out on the other side quite unscathed. Once again the angel smiled, and led me into yet another cave, dark, drear, and I thought at first empty, but soon I perceived a stout wooden pillar rising from a smooth slab, stained with blood. Suddenly the old fear returned. I remembered what the angel had said about the suffering not being over. I tried to hold on to my new confidence, but fear surged through me as I stood, gazing about me. The angel had disappeared for a few moments but now he came back looking grave, and carrying with him a stout chain and a heavily knotted scourge. He told me to kneel down on the blood-stained slab, then, lifting my hands above my head, he chained them to the pillar and scourged me unmercifully until my blood joined that already staining the slab. At last I was unchained, and the angel led me down a dark passage, out of the cave to where we looked out on to a dreary wilderness of rocks with a few shrubs growing here and there. He told me to sit at the doorway of the cave and to await a terrifying experience. If my confidence was such that I could face the experience unflinchingly, then all would be well, but each time that I returned to the safety of the cave I should be scourged and should have to begin again until I learned the lesson of absolute confidence. Then the angel left me. As I sat there I saw strange shapes rise from the wilderness. Gradually they came nearer and nearer, enormous lions—and following them those eternal lizards, bigger and more terrifying than ever before. As they came nearer I could bear the terror no longer. I fled screaming into the cave where the angel was waiting sadly, the scourge in his hand. Three times in all I fled back into the cave, and three more times I was scourged. As I sat at the cave door for the fourth time, a new determination enveloped me, mingled with a feeling of great depression and also one of entire detachment. What did it matter whether I lived or died? I was as nothing, as a grain of dust, not worthy of the privilege of life. I let the beasts advance in all their horror, not caring what they might do to me—but, surprisingly enough, as they saw me facing them so calmly a wonderful thing happened. The lizards disappeared and the lions became calm and lay down at my feet. "Why," I thought, exulting, "They're my slaves for evermore." As I sat there savouring this new success, the angel appeared—and, joy of joys, with him was the snake! I greeted him with ecstasy, the angel smiled, and I looked at him, and where there had been hate there now came into my being the wonderful warm sensation of love. "Come, my child," said the angel, "the suffering is over, let us go and seek the joy together. You have learned the lessons of true humility, trust, confidence, and above all (smiling gently as he read my feelings in my face) of love. Come, there is yet greater joy to be found."

'I followed him back into the cave with the snake coming behind. We passed through the cave where I had been scourged and on into another, larger cave. This cave was diffused with green light and all around in a gallery there were angels singing beautiful soft music. On the left of the cave was a sort of altar, with three angels above it, their arms folded across their breasts. Candles were burning on each side of the altar and in the middle were three silver dishes. To the right of the cave, gushing forth from the rock, was a spring where the angel bade me go and wash. As I did so, the wounds on my back were immediately healed and I felt a new physical vitality surging within me. When I had washed the angel gave me a new robe—far less beautiful than the one I had been given so long ago, but when I had put it on, I knew I should learn to prefer it. It was the coarse, white shift of a penitent. Now the angel bade me kneel before him, and as I did so he shaved my head, annointed it with oil, then covered it with a coarse white veil. The angel now took me by the hand and led me to the altar, where I knelt down. As I did so, the singing of the angels in the gallery ceased. The angel who had been with me all the journey stood behind me and the snake was at my side. The angels above the altar lifted up the three silver dishes and put each one in turn to my lips. The first contained milk, the second honey, and the third salt. After I had partaken of each dish, the angels in the gallery started to sing again, this time a joyful hymn of praise.

'The angel took me by the hand, gave me a candle and led me to the other side of the cave. Before us was a long dark passage. It was very narrow, but down it we all went, the angel leading and the snake coming behind. The only light was from my candle which showed rocky walls, running with moisture. The passage was tortuous, always narrow, now rising steeply, now going downhill. We kept on for hours and hours. Soon the snake wound himself round my waist. I was glad; it was a comfort to have him there. Still we kept on—seemingly for days. Just as every step was becoming agony, and I thought I should faint from weariness, we went sharply down-hill and then suddenly we began to fall, slowly and gently in a floating kind of way. We went on falling for ages until it seemed we must meet the centre of the earth, down, down and down. I felt a curious sense of peace about me, though, and I was not at all frightened. Now we landed gently, seemingly at the bottom of a deep well. To the left a passage led off, dark and narrow like the first, and all the time going sharply downhill. Again we walked down this passage for a very long time. I seemed to have been walking in the dark for a lifetime, when suddenly before us there was a blazing light which almost blinded us for a few moments. When we became accustomed to the light, we saw that we were at the entrance to a great cavern, guarded by two fierce-looking dragons. "Go in," the angel told me, and, without hesitating, I walked past the guardians of the gate, who, seeing that I was calm and unafraid, made no attempt to stop me. The angel followed. The cave was the most beautiful place I have ever seen. All around were plants, pools, stalagmites, stalactites, great glowing jewels which made the blazing light, and the whole was filled with a rich angelic music which echoed round and round. I could only stand and wonder at the glory before me. After a while, the angel told me to proceed, and I did so, passing from this cave to another even more beautiful. In all, we passed through ten of these wonderful caverns.

'Then we came to the eleventh. Words cannot describe the beauty of this—I fell down and wept, I was so moved. The angel gently bade me rise and look around me, which I did. Everywhere there was light, colour and jewels—but suddenly I was struck by the perfection of form in the cave. It was hexagonal in shape. In every section of the hexagon stood an angelic choir bathed in coloured light—a different colour for each section, and each one surrounded by the most breath-taking beauty in rock formation and plants. They were singing most wonderful music. The roof of the cave was a dome, with six sections, and everywhere there was perfectly formed vaulting made up of hexagonal shapes. In the centre of the cave was a beautifully carved fountain, the different coloured lights playing on its fine, mist-like spray. This fountain, too, was shaped like a hexagon. The angel led me to the fountain and bade me thrust my hand into the middle of the spray, and then take out what I should find there. As I stretched out my hand, the music stopped—all was expectation. I closed my hand round something hard and perfect in form; I brought it out into the light and, as I gazed at this beautiful thing in awe, the angelic choirs sang a triumphant chorus, and all around me I could hear whispered the words "the Deep Centre, the Deep Centre". (I've read those words somewhere—I believe they are a Jungian term but I'm not sure of their exact significance.) The object in my hand was a jewel of very great beauty, yellow in colour. It had six sides and on each side it was cut in myriad hexagonal shapes. It was about as big as a tea-cup and it gave out the most wonderful coloured lights. I could have gazed at it for ever. The angel smiled at my wonderment; "Keep it carefully, my child, this is the Deep Centre, the transforming symbol, by which from now onwards you will live your life. Life is a beautiful thing and having found this Deep Centre, this transforming symbol, you will be enabled to live it fully and in depth."

'Then holding the jewel, and wondering all the time, the snake and the angel and myself walked together out of this marvellous cave, and through ten more like the first ten. We passed safely by two more dragons and up another dark passage—very steep like the one we had come down to reach the caves. When we got to the top we found ourselves in another tunnel with a river flowing to the right. On the river was a kind of canoe which we got into and began to drift slowly, slowly down the passage towards the right.'

When the summer term began, Ruth was still largely in her inner world, finding it difficult to adjust to the demands of College work and even to the impact of surrounding scenery. More real to her was the slow drifting with the snake and the angel along the underground stream, the rock walls wet with moisture. This journey continued every night. Nothing was said, but Ruth was quite content.

As she was clearly coming back into the outer world, I discussed with her the possibility of relying on the angel and on her link with the Deep Centre for help with the outer practical problems that were impinging more and more in her final term of teacher-training. I had a strong inner directive, myself, to emphasise the two-way flow between inner and outer at this transitional point. The next four chapters show how the links were made and applied to different aspects of living. But first the last part of the journey which she brought in writing during May:

'We went on and on, floating, floating, for ages and ages, down the river. Eventually we came to a kind of stone slab jutting out into the river; the angel moored the boat to a ring in the stone, and told us to leave the boat and follow him. We did so and found ourselves in a very narrow passage—pitch dark and winding its way up and up. We soon had to get on hands and knees and practically drag ourselves along, so narrow and steep was the tunnel. Every movement was agony and the tunnel was seemingly without end—but still we must go on and on, further and further into the inky blackness. My hands were cut and my body grazed as I searched for holds in the rock and dragged myself on and on. Yet always beyond the pain, the struggle to keep going, was the feeling that a fount of strength and determination far greater than anything I possessed was impelling me onwards to some goal, and it was this feeling which made the struggle acceptable, the suffering bearable.

'After a very long time, a great wind blew down the tunnel, and, looking ahead, we could see light. There was still far to go, but the goal was at least in sight. Now the tunnel became wider and went upwards far less steeply. Soon we could stand again and walk quite naturally, tired as we were, on and on towards the light.

Still the wind was blowing strongly and always the light was coming nearer and nearer, until at last the passage opened out into a large cave. Here, once again, there was a spring, and the angel bade me rest and drink from the pure clear water gushing forth from the rock. This I did and soon passed into a deep, tranquil, relaxed sleep where all the fatigue of the journey was forgotten, and from which I awoke refreshed, and dressed, to my surprise, no longer in a shift, but in a gay red cotton frock, as if I were dressed for a party. All around there seemed to be an air of expectancy and the angel and the snake were waiting for me to follow them. As soon as I was fully awake, they led me to the entrance to the cave, through which brilliant sunlight poured. The cave looked out on to a scene of very great beauty—a woodland glade, where birds sang, rabbits played, a stream flowed gaily past and the sun shone gentle and warm through the delicate green leaves of trees in springtime. As we stood admiring the peace and beauty of the scene, two shadows appeared dancing in the sunlit glade—one purple—that of the snake—and one blue—my own. As they danced, they came closer and closer together; they danced more and more in harmony until suddenly they joined together as one and disappeared as suddenly as they had come. I had a momentary feeling of uneasiness and looked down at the snake—but he no longer lay by my side—he had gone. Suddenly my uneasiness passed and I realized that the snake and I, like the shadows, were truly one at last. I turned to the angel who took my hands in his. "Go," he said, "the journey is over. You have learned much. Take your knowledge into life and teach others, always remembering that I am here within you—a great source of strength which you can contact at will—and that you carry with you the perfect jewel, the transforming symbol: the reminder of the Deep Centre."

'So, smiling steadfastly at the angel, and holding the jewel with great care, I stepped from the cave into the glade. I knew that this was life, and life was wonderful.'

CHAPTER 3

Balance and Relationship

May to November 1958

Balancing Inner and Outer Worlds

After the first journey had ended, the dreams ceased for a while. But I began to consult the angel about my inability to concentrate on my studies, and I wrote down what he said:

'It is only natural that your strongest pull at the moment should be towards the inner world—but you must remember that in the inner world you have learned courage—and it is courage, determination and strength which you must now bring to the problem of this conflict between "inner" and "outer". The inner world may be more attractive, but you cannot live there alone. You must learn to bring all you have learned there to help you in the life of the outer world.

'First, learn to accept the situation as it is at the moment. After such a long period in the inner world, with such intense activity, you cannot hope to turn your whole concentration outwards suddenly. There must be a time factor and you must realize and provide for this. Allow a certain time each day for "inner communion", when you will gain strength from the Deep Centre. Feel that you can trust life. Let yourself be lived from the depths instead of fretting over trifles. Do not forget that I am always here, to help and to guide, that in a few moments of quietness you can find me, and in me whatever you need in order to face the situation in hand.

'Do not expect too much of yourself. When you know you can't concentrate for long on one thing, provide for a frequent change of occupation, and gradually, as inner and outer become integrated, you will find concentration perhaps even better than before. Above all, do not expect everything to happen at once. You were a long time in the inner world, and it may take even longer for your experiences to work out in the outer world. Be very patient and all will work out in its own time.'

I also asked the angel to help with a friend's problem. He did give advice, but added: 'Try yourself not to become too emotionally involved in another's problems, for then you will see nothing in its right perspective, and you will be a help neither to B. nor to yourself. Again, remember I am here, always ready to help.'

Soon dreams began again, this time of a kind designed to teach by images. For example, I fell asleep thinking about religion and the new attitude which I must take to it in view of my experiences in the inner world. In a dream the angel came to me and took me to a field where a man was sowing seed. When the field was sown, the rain came, then the sun, then snow and wind, more rain and more sun. Now the seed grew up into a field of corn, tall straight and golden, and shearers came and reaped the harvest, and when the stubble was left the field was ploughed and sown again. 'Now do you understand? asked the angel. 'The coming of truth to the human mind is like a series of harvests, of ploughing and sowing, and it is but gradually that you will come to that truth which you will know is wholly right for you. Be patient.'

A few days later the angel said: 'It is not in your own interest at this particular time that I should answer your questions. If you give too much of yourself to such speculation and meditation, you will not have the energy which is so necessary to you, at the moment, in the outer world. The examination and assessment period is very close, and your whole energy must be devoted at present to your work. I will help you to do this, but you must co-operate by coming to me only at the time which you set aside for "inner communion"—and even then you must come not to ask questions but to gain refreshment and strength. The time *will* come when you will be free to enter the world of meditation, but until then you must try to put questions away from you, and to think only on such a level as will benefit you in the outer world. I know that it is difficult, for you are not really ready for such a cold "return", but you know that with the strength of the Deep Centre all is possible.'

The following dream was repeated three times. I was on a kind of plateau, not very high up, but from where I stood I could not see over the edge. I was digging in the loose soil on the plateau, trying desperately, with my bare hands, to reach some depth, but wherever I tried the soil was only a few inches deep and I soon came to solid rock. Suddenly the angel appeared and bade me stop digging and follow him. I did so, and he led me to the edge of the plateau where I could see people at work making hay, reaping corn, sowing seed, and others riding horses in the sunshine. Looking beyond the fields where all this was happening, I saw a village bustling with life. I followed the angel and we climbed down from the plateau, walked at a leisurely pace through the fields, and eventually came to the village. There was no main street, and from the number of people it seemed like market day but there was no market to be seen. At the end of the street was a dirty, ramshackle old cottage, which we entered and went upstairs. In the shadows stood an old desk, with yellow parchment on it and a quill pen. The angel told me to sit down quietly and write. I was about to do so but was consumed with a sudden desire to return to the plateau. I ran outside where I found a horse tethered. I jumped on it and rode towards the plateau which I could see quite clearly, but though I rode until I was exhausted, the plateau came no nearer, and I got off the horse only to find that we had not moved away from the dirty cottage. I tied the horse up again and went wearily upstairs, where the angel stood—waiting. I sat down at the desk, took the quill pen, and began to write, but my tears blurred the ink, and, as I was going to read what I had written, I woke up.

In trying to understand the dream, I felt that the soil stood for the inner life, and digging meant finding inner truths. I wanted to dig below the rock and felt that the angel had put the rock there so that I could not dig. Examinations were imminent, and preparation for them needed all my energy.

In another dream I was with the angel in a cart with two horses pulling it. The angel was driving. We were driving round the edge of a wood. Suddenly the angel handed the reins to me and told me to drive. Not content to keep to the wide cart-track at the edge of the wood, I took a narrow path which led towards the middle. The trees and undergrowth became thicker, and soon it was impossible to take the cart any further. Possessed now by a terrible urge to reach the centre of the wood, I jumped out of the cart and pushed my way through the ever-thickening growth, not heeding my torn clothes or the bruises and cuts over my body. At last, with a great effort, I reached my goal—the centre of the wood—where there was a clearing thickly girt with trees, and in the middle of the clearing a clear pond.

Suddenly the pond dried up and the ground began to quake and tremble. I was paralysed with fear, then, seized with sudden panic, I tried to run, but the way was barred by the thickness of the wood and by falling trees. Then I felt a calming hand on my shoulder, and the angel, who had followed me, said, 'Remember, you can do everything in the strength of the Deep Centre.' I was calm, then suddenly was filled with indescribable strength, and with great ease I uprooted or tossed aside trees in order to clear a pathway through the woods. When I reached the edge again, the cart was waiting, and the angel was still behind me. We both got in, and the angel pointed ahead to a long, straight and narrow road. 'Drive on,' he said, and I did so.

In interpreting, I felt that the wood on the left represented the inner world; the barren landscape to the right was the outer world. I wanted to dive deeply into the inner, and the problem was that of keeping to the Middle Way.

In my last interview with Dr. Swainson before I left College, the angel was present, standing behind my chair. Dr. Swainson asked if he had any message for her. I 'tuned in' for a moment and then told her, 'He just says, "Thank you".' So she also said, 'Thank you.'

In the summer vacation I heard the news that I had passed my examinations, though until I saw it in print I didn't believe it! I wrote to Dr. Swainson:

'You yourself are aware, I know, of the tremendous change

which has come over me since I started seeing you last October. I feel so happy, so full of vitality, so content with life, able to live it "in depth"—a "whole" human being instead of a very frightened piece of one—and, as you know, I have found something which is indescribably precious.'

And later :

'The angel has been discouraging my attempts at excursions into the "inner world", and gradually I am learning to accept and to respect his judgment. In one of those "day dreams" he took me into a thick forest, which we penetrated with difficulty until we came to a clearing in the middle. Here there was a small dark pond. The angel picked up a large stone and dropped it into the pond. From the way the stone fell, I gathered that the pond was extremely deep. Then the angel spoke : "This pond is of unknown and immeasurable depth. If you could learn to enjoy life in the outer world and to recognize its value, the pond would be symbolic of the life available to you in the inner world, but the two lives are complementary and until you learn to achieve and value a balance between the two, the life on either side will be limited."

'One thing still worries me (although I know it shouldn't because I realize how lucky I am really) and that is the vividness of these experiences. To tell you about them is an enormous relief, but sometimes I wonder if I am mad, and I know that many people would think I was. I sometimes feel so lonely, and somehow "apart", and turning to the angel doesn't help—it just adds to these strange experiences. Yet with the biggest part of me I never cease to marvel that I should be allowed to have such wonderful experiences.'

The Lizards, the Snake, and Relationship

In September this dream came twice :

Once more I stood outside the cave where I had been scourged; the lions (now my slaves) lay at my feet, but from the wilderness arose once more the dread shapes of the lizards. Now I must show that I was stronger than they. They did not stir up the old shrinking fear within me; my fear was now more positive, I was terrified but determined to win my way through. I turned to the angel (who was at my side) for advice. He handed me a sword and shield and I understood that I must conquer by fighting. Then ensued a terrible battle. I was wounded, frightened, desperate, but always some indescribable force drove me to strike and strike again. As we fought, the ground beneath my feet became soft, and I was reminded of the mud where I had first met the lizards. I began to sink but still I fought with every ounce of my energy and now I was encouraged by the sight of the biggest and most fearsome lying dead near by. I struggled from the mud on to a piece of firm ground near by, and there, having an advantage over the enemy, I fought until the last creature lay dead at my feet, then I dropped exhausted beside the angel. He took my hand, and a new vitality flowed through me. I got up and was well rewarded for my fight by the approving smile which the angel gave me, but a strong wind had arisen and I began to shiver with cold. The angel threw a purple cloak about my shoulders, and said, 'The wind, as you know from experience, is the symbol which purifies and wipes clean, and this purple cloak which you may now wear is the cloak of the conqueror. It is yet another symbol to remind you that in the inner world you have learned courage, and if you are patient and wait always for the strength which comes from the Deep Centre, and try all by the transforming symbol, then you can bring the full force of this inner strength to all problems and conflicts in the outer world. Always I remain your Guide.'

As the deep inner experiences began to work out in the outer world, I noticed an improvement in my eyesight. I think I first noticed this in the classroom, one day, when I had written something on the blackboard. I wandered round to the back of the classroom and was surprised that from there I could read quite clearly what I had written. (From September I had taken a teaching post in a village school.) I noticed the improvement even more startlingly when, on sitting in the back row at an evening class, I found I could read the lecturer's small writing with ease, even though the room was lit by somewhat inefficient artificial light. The sight in my right eye had not improved, but the sight in my left eye was definitely stronger, and I no longer suffered from eye-strain after working for long periods.

The next problem to be dealt with was that of human relationships, particularly with the opposite sex. Here I had long discussions with the angel and also, more specifically, with the snake, who was very helpful.

I dreamed that I was in a tiny boat in the middle of the ocean, with the angel and the snake. Suddenly a great storm blew up and every wave threatened to capsize our fragile craft. At last, when I felt I could hold on no longer, an island came in sight, but we were still a long way from it when the boat started to drift back the way we had come, still pitching and tossing alarmingly. With one accord, we flung ourselves from the boat into the raging seas and with a last desperate effort gained the island— which was little more than a rock in the middle of the ocean— and sank down exhausted. Hardly had we reached the island than the storm began to abate, then came a great calm. The snake no longer sat apart from me, but we became one again. Previously he had been curled up inside me, in front, his head just at the top of my chest. But now he took up a different position, twisted round me, outside.

Whilst on holiday in Lancashire I took a solitary walk to the highest spot in Darwen—a part of the Pennine Chain, where stands a monument to Queen Victoria's reign, a tower. In the town there was a slight fog, but up on the moors all was clear and one looked down, surprisingly enough, not at the grime-caked chimney-stacks of the industrial north, but at a swirling white sea of cloud. I was alone and cut off, with only the angel as a companion, but I sensed no loneliness, only a deep encompassing tranquillity. I climbed to the top of the tower where there was far less wind than on the hill-top, and I stood for a while gazing and wondering at the quality of the scene. Suddenly and without warning I had a strange and beautiful experience which words cannot describe. Time ceased to exist, and I, as a being, was not; all things were woven together in a kind of spiritual unity, and all was peace.

How long the experience lasted I do not know, but it left me mentally a little dazed; yet as I was walking back home all the doubts and fears about a personal problem which had, that morning, been nagging at my mind, had vanished.

Later, in a dream, I was with the angel in a wild and desolate kind of wilderness, and I was completely enveloped in a coarse, not very transparent veil. The angel told me to take the veil off, which I did. Suddenly, with the lifting of the veil, the wilderness was transformed; it was no longer desolate and rocky but beautiful green foliage abounded, the sun shone and there was a marvellous sense of peace and completeness, as in a beautiful garden on a drowsy summer's day.

I asked the angel about the meaning of this dream, and he told me that the lifting of the veil was symbolic of what I must attempt in outer-world relationships—the lifting of the veil of over-timidity and shyness.

In another dream I stood on the banks of a wide and swiftly flowing river, but on the opposite bank stood the angel. I desperately wanted to reach him, but the only means of crossing the river was by a tightrope. I started off on this perilous journey but soon began to wobble hopelessly. Suddenly the snake appeared, as if suspended from above, and offered himself as a hold with which to steady myself. I refused his offer and continued to struggle alone, but then I began to fall and in desperation, reaching for the snake, suddenly realized how foolish I was to struggle alone, whereupon with the snake's help I soon reached the opposite bank and was at last reunited with the angel.

Again I dreamed that I stood before a glass cupboard in which the snake was locked (or so it appeared). I tried frantically to reach the snake, shaking and battering at the cupboard to no avail. Suddenly the angel appeared with a single command: 'Relax.' I took no notice of him, but continued to try to open the cupboard by force. The angel watched with a sorrowful expression on his face. Then I was overcome by a great wearinesss. I turned in utter wretchedness to the angel who took me by the hand and led me to a grassy meadow where all was green and peaceful— a source of spiritual strength. There I lay for a while and relaxed. Suddenly my gaze fell on a rock, and I remembered that I had been once before to this meadow, and had hidden a key beneath that rock. Intuitively I knew that here was the key to the cupboard. I went to the rock, the key was still there, and I took it and ran, followed by the angel, back to the cupboard. The key fitted easily in the lock, and immediately the snake was free. The angel had one comment to offer : 'Now do you understand that outer-world battles can best be fought with inner strength?'

CHAPTER 4

The Monsters and the Octopus

Christmas 1958 to March 1959

The Monsters of Pride

Ever since Christmas, and throughout January, this dream was repeated continually:

I was walking down a country lane (the road I go along to school) with the angel, when, in a field, we saw some children. When they saw the angel they stopped their game and ran to ask him to tell them a story. This he did sitting down on the grass, and afterwards he talked to them for a while. When the children wanted to resume their game, they invited both the angel and me to join in with them, but I resented the time which the angel had spent with the children, and was furious that they should make this further demand on him. I wanted to continue our walk and to have the angel to myself once more. Suddenly I could contain my fury no longer. I struck at the children, hitting many of them; at first they thought this was some kind of game, but soon they realized that my anger and violence were very real, and they ran away screaming and frightened. When they had gone, my anger was still not entirely spent and I flung myself down, tearing up great pieces of turf, flinging them away, kicking and screaming until, utterly exhausted, I fell asleep. When I woke, I remembered these happenings with a great sense of shame; I hardly dared to look to see if the angel were still there. He was, and when he saw that I was awake, he took my hand, and led me to the road without a word. It was now getting dark, but we continued our walk, in silence, for a long time. Suddenly ahead there was a great light—very beautiful, like full moonlight in summer, only much brighter—and on the left side of the road we could see the gates to a park, guarded by a small naked child. I wanted to go into the park, but the child, on seeing my face, closed the gate. Beyond I could see streams, flowers, trees, and all kinds of wild life moving about openly and fearlessly. It seemed to be a place of profound peace. 'Let me in,' I said somewhat haughtily to the child guardian, but he shook his head. 'First you must receive a little child.' 'Why?' I exclaimed, the former anger returning once more, 'I'll kill you, you horrid brat,' and would have done so, but the child gazed at me steadfastly, the light became too brilliant, I was dazzled and my feet seemed to be stuck to the ground. I turned my back on the light and then began to run from the place, along the road which we had been walking along before. I ran and ran until I came to a wood. I plunged into it regardless of the tangled undergrowth and briars, and soon fell flat. I had no will to get up again but lay there, all anger gone, once more ashamed and miserable. There the angel came to me, but still I would not get up. He sat down beside me, and began to talk to me gently, rather as one might talk to a naughty child, sulking after its punishment.

'Why don't you get up and let's get out of this wood, where we can talk comfortably? You can't stay here for ever, and a good talk will probably put things right. You could tell me all about it, couldn't you?'

'All about what?'

'Why you were so angry with the children and with the guardian.'

I could not bring myself to co-operate, and it was not until mid-February that I felt able to have a long, personal talk with the angel. He referred to my own early childhood, presenting me with scenes of which I had no recollection. My feelings of shame and guilt were so painful that I could hardly look at them, finding it very difficult to follow the angel's complete understanding and acceptance of the child that I was. Later, he told me to cling to the Deep Centre and the jewel, and gave me a sword for the battle with my pride, but the sword was so heavy that I could not lift it.

Throughout the rest of the month I had a series of acute nightmares. In the first I was beneath the sea, in the clutches of a great octopus. I was armed with the angel's sword. While I remained calm, I had a certain amount of freedom within the tentacles of the octopus, bent around me like a cave, but as soon as I struggled to be free, the tentacles grasped me in a strangling grip. The only means of escape would be to cut myself free but still I could not lift the sword.

The second nightmare was one I realized I used to have frequently as a child but had since forgotten. Bands of different colours passed before me as if mounted on a revolving wheel, together with a mounting tension, anxiety and terror, and a terrible drumming in the ears. Suddenly a band of black appeared, dreadful to behold, seething and bubbling itself into a great blister. I was terrified that this blister would burst. Suddenly a pin appeared, and as the blister burst I woke up, terrified and shaking.

On the third consecutive night of this nightmare, when I awoke shaking, the angel came after a while and took my hand, gently soothing me into tranquil sleep. In the morning I awoke refreshed to find the angel still sitting on the bed beside me. For some reason or other I could find nothing better to say to him than, 'What is your name? You have never told me and I should like to know.'

'Gildas,' he replied, 'You may call me that if you wish; remember that I am here to help you, I will comfort you when you are wounded, and renew your strength when you are faint-hearted, but it is you who must fight the battle, and when you are ready to pour out the deep hatred inside you, I shall be here to listen, for I am always with you. The battle, I am afraid, will be long; you will be tried to the utmost, you will want to give up; but go on, remembering always that you are far more fortunate than many, for you have the strength of the Deep Centre and the jewel, and you know from experience that the joy will exceed the pain.'

Now there were no nights without one or other of the two nightmares. If I woke up, the angel was there to comfort and soothe me, but he also looked a little anxious, as though waiting for something. Eventually, in a deep trough of depression and unhappiness, I sought the comfort of Gildas but didn't get it.

'So you have come to me at last. Are you ready to work off some of the hatred?'

'No—oh no, I can't possibly do that yet; I'm so miserable, I've no energy, no will to do anything. This fight takes up so much vitality.'

'Listen, Ruth, carefully; when you have been through other struggles I have always been there, haven't I, to comfort and guide and renew strength?'

'Yes.'

'Well, so I should be this time, my dear, if you were using your vitality for fighting, but you're not. You're wallowing in this trough of misery—enjoying it really. That energy is not going into the fight but into the wholly useless operation of building a stronger shell with which to wall in your repressed hatred. Now, lift that sword I gave you and clear the path to freedom.'

'But the sword is so heavy, Gildas; I am not strong enough, and I'm so frightened.'

'Your fear I have sympathy with, but the plea of not being strong enough is wholly false, and you know it! These tests are not given until you are strong enough. If you wish to continue with the inner work you *must* co-operate.'

I complained that there were too many other demands on my time and energy. Gildas promised that no inner demands would be made during the hours when I was teaching, but he asked me to keep a regular time each night when we could work together to break down the defences. He would prefer at least an hour, but half an hour would do, if I were prepared to work hard.

'That's far too long, it's impossible.'

'Ruth! This piece of work, when finished, will give you an entirely new field of freedom, something which will affect your whole life and work—and then you say that half an hour a day is too much time to be spent. I hope you know what you are doing, for in denying me this time, you take yourself beyond my power to help you. If you wish to change your mind, I shall be waiting, but *you* must come to *me*. I shall pray for you, for I hate to see you fall by the wayside now !'

'Oh for goodness sake stop preaching and leave me alone. I shan't fall by the wayside, in fact I'll probably manage a good deal better on my own, using *my* methods instead of listening to *your* advice which leads to so much struggle and pain. I've had enough, and least of all do I need prayers from you or anyone else. I can manage without help.'

That night I was pursued by an evil monster—one of those prehistoric things with a sail on its back. I ran terrified over rocky ground, but a female monster, accompanied by its young one, came rushing towards me. In terror I turned to the side and ran and ran, still hotly pursued by the three sail-backed monsters. Suddenly I tripped and fell into a seemingly bottomless abyss. All was dark as I fell, and I was still falling when I awoke feeling very frightened and panic-stricken, especially with no angel to call upon. This nightmare was repeated until, after three days and nights of terror, lack of ability to concentrate, and deep feelings of tremendous guilt, shame and self-loathing, I finally admitted to myself that I desperately needed the help of the angel—Gildas. He was near, I could feel his presence, but it was though he were behind a wall of glass, powerless to come to me. If I went to him the barrier would disappear, I knew, but I had a dreadful fore-boding of some painful work ahead, and it was certainly not easy to find the humility which I knew I must have in order to ask the forgiveness of Gildas. Thus it was only after more painful conflict that I finally resolved to approach him. I acted on that resolution immediately before I could change my mind, but even so, my first words were very stiff and somewhat ungracious.

'I was wrong, Gildas. I am not strong enough alone. I will try to co-operate if you will help me.'

'I am glad you have seen reason at last. I have been longing to help you, for it is my eternal task to guide you, to be with you and help you, to love and comfort you, and it has grieved me to see you turning from the Way. You realize, of course, that what I said about those defences was true, and that we must tackle them now, don't you? And that the loss of time has made the task more difficult?'

'Yes, I think I do, but first of all, please, tell me what the dreadful monster nightmare meant. It is the most horrible nightmare I've ever had.'

'That, actually, was one of your main defences invading you, Ruth, and it is the defence which you must tackle first. Those monsters are the monsters of pride. You had thought of your pride as a god (with feet of clay it is true) but it's not, you see; it's still very primitive and uncontrolled and as likely to guide you, to invade you, as it is to allow itself to be moulded the way you wish it to go. A *little* pride in human nature is an excellent thing, and is known as self-respect; for that reason you have no need to fear the baby monster, but the two big monsters you must kill with my sword before they breed other offspring and invade you completely. You even had to battle with them, didn't you, before you could re-approach me? If you learn to use the small monster properly, he will turn into something far less primitive, perhaps a cat—a self-respecting animal—but one which is also to a degree lovable.'

'I am too frightened—and I really *can't* lift that sword.'

'You learned to conquer fear, Ruth, in the inner world. All those experiences on the journey to find the Deep Centre were given you to enable you later to fight for the wholeness of your personality. That time is here now. You have scratched the surface of some problems before, but now is the time to tackle them on a deeper and more permanent level, and remember that the inner forces are never wrong in their timing and estimations. You have numerous battles to fight yet, and the process of integration continues for many years. What you must aim at, at this particular stage of development, is freedom—freedom from false ideals, opinions, attitudes, values—freedom to live your life as an individual with self-confidence and security, instead of as an insecure practitioner of attitudes which for you are meaningless. You have all the inner strength you will ever need. Much has been given to you, and much will be expected from you in return. Some things will finally solve themselves at a deep unconscious level, as with your attitude to sex, but that does not mean that there will be no suffering, no battle, no monsters first. There are infinite rewards for those who achieve integration, but first they must learn through pain and struggle. And so, my dear, though it may be difficult, you must cling to the jewel and draw strength from the Deep Centre with which to lift the sword. You have so much inner strength if only you will learn to use it instead of being so aggressively independent and trying things in that surface strength which has no roots. The slaying of the monsters of pride will help you there as well.'

'You explain things so beautifully for me—thank you. Can I attempt the slaying of the monsters now, do you think, using active imagination?'

'I think it would be a good idea to use active imagination to pick up the threads of the nightmare and to slay the monsters. But one word of warning: the experience will be very painful, for your monsters of pride are very real, and in a strange way, underneath, you have a curious affection for them. Their death agonies will strike a chord of deep pain in you. For years you have leaned upon and used pride to carry you through all kinds of situations in life and it is truly a part of you, but one which must, to a large extent, die. I shall be here with you, but I can assure you that this will not be an easy test of your strength.'

Using active imagination, I took the nightmare from the point where, after having been pursued by the male monster, I was suddenly confronted by the female and her offspring.

I was terrified on seeing this new threat to my safety, but knew that if I turned and ran in another direction I should only fall into the bottomless abyss. With a conscious effort I stopped running, and was about to summon the strength required to wield the angel's sword which now appeared beside me, when I saw also a club-shaped piece of rock. Thinking the latter weapon might be easier to manage, I seized it and turned, desperately afraid, to face the monsters, now terribly close. (At this point it was difficult to sustain the phantasy as I was experiencing feelings on two levels: the inner terror, but, far worse, an outer panic.) With difficulty I shut out the outer world and struck out blindly at the monsters with my club, then peeping apprehensively, I

73

saw the two big monsters lying stunned on some horribly muddy ground. I burst into tears and the phantasy ended.

Gildas was with me, as he had promised, but realizing that I was completely exhausted and upset, he gave me some practical advice.

'Well, there's quite a lot to say about that, but you are tired now. Make a hot drink and go to bed. Come to me again to-morrow evening and we'll see if we can sort out things then.'

I got into bed, and Gildas was with me compelling me to relax, and I soon fell asleep. The nightmare with the monsters was repeated in the form it had taken before my attempt at active imagination. Once more the angel soothed me to sleep.

The following evening I came again to Gildas. 'Well, what do I have to do now?'

He spoke gravely. 'I'm afraid we haven't progressed far enough to go on to the next stage yet. Your "phantasy" which exhausted you so last night was no solution to the problem. You only *stunned* the monsters, you must *kill* them however painful it is; they are choking you and arresting your progress. My sword is *the only weapon* for the task. Do not allow yourself to be attracted into using something else. The stunning blow from the club will not remain effective for long; the monsters will "come round" when you least expect it and you will be powerless to control them. All that mud too! We shall have to deal with that as well, but first things first. Are you going to have another attempt at the monsters?'

'I suppose so, but really I did try; oh dear, I feel as if I could give up at every turn in the pathway!'

'Now don't hide yourself behind those feelings of depression again! Stand up and face the battle. It will be well worth it in the end, you know.'

'All right, I'll try.'

Once more I picked up the threads of the nightmare, using active imagination. This time, with terrific effort, I succeeded in wielding the angel's sword and killing the parent monsters, though I seemed to feel all the agony of their death myself. Afterwards, gazing at the lifeless carcasses, and the extremely docile-looking one of the baby monster, I felt utterly empty and devastated. But Gildas came into the phantasy, took my hand and led me near to the dead creatures. At first I was frightened, but then I saw why he had led me to that spot. In the great muddy print of one of the monsters' feet grew a flower of pure gold. It rose from a rosette of six gold leaves and had six petals, resembling a hexagon, and a trumpet like a daffodil. It was perfect in form and was indescribably beautiful. I looked at this thing in awe and turned to Gildas for an explanation.

'It is the flower of humility,' he said. 'Cherish it and plant it in richer soil than it has here, and it will be with you always, one of your most valued possessions.'

Later he said, 'Well, at last you have done it. I know you feel as if you have a deep wound yourself at the moment, but as you learn to care for your golden flower, your wound will heal. You still have the small monster, but you must look after him too; it would never do for him to grow into a big monster. Be patient with him, train him to society until gradually he takes on a more civilized form and becomes more amenable. Now you deserve a good night's rest, but remember there is still a great deal of work to be done.'

The Octopus

Now that the monsters of pride were dead I was able to express some of my repressed hatred in writing. But the angel showed me that it came out in the form of cold bitterness. 'Where,' he asked, 'is all the fury, the white-hot screaming rage of resentment?'

I begged for time, but he advised me not to wait too long. Meanwhile I was never free from nightmares, either of the octopus or the colour-bands. Night after night I had one or the other.

'Oh Gildas, I feel exhausted and devastated. Suddenly life is meaningless—an almost intolerable burden which I haven't the energy to carry. I feel as if I can't begin to face my sinfulness, or the octopus, or to untie that horrible knot of "white-hot fury hatred". Help me to put these feelings aside and to find the energy to go on. What is the next step anyway?'

'Why must you always assume that inconvenient feelings must

be "put aside"? It is extremely rare when this is the best policy, you know! If you have such feelings, it is better to face them and find out *why* you have them, not to "put them aside" and leave them free to weave a horrid mesh in which to trap you when you least expect it. You feel so exhausted because your mind is full of such negative thoughts. And of course you feel devastated and see life as meaningless after your battle with the monsters; you've killed something which you had nourished and tended carefully for years, and as yet you have not accepted the golden flower as its replacement. But I assure you this is a phase which will pass. Meanwhile it might be a good idea to do some *positive* thinking about the goal of life—your personal goal I mean, not the re-hash of someone else's goal. As for these negative thoughts, they need replacing, or rather to be absorbed by positive material. If you will sit quietly and try to empty your mind, and then to visualize the positive symbols—the golden flower, the jewel, the beautiful fountain where you found the jewel—I think you will find that so long as you don't shut the negative thoughts out completely, you will face them with more strength, and calm —but nevertheless powerful—energy, and they will take on a different light.

'As for the next step, it is two-fold: you must free yourself from the octopus and let out all the fury.'

'Yes, that worries me too—the fury. Now that the path is clearer and I can see it and feel it too, I realize just how powerful it is; it's like a live thing, like a tightly rolled piece of elastic threatening to tear me in shreds if I once allow it to spring undone. I am beginning even to *want* to let it out, but *how*? It's far too big to be expressed in words; they are so inadequate for things like this.'

'Why don't you try painting or dancing? Or playing some especially loud piece of music? That would help, and words might come later. You could do a wonderful dance-drama of a bad temper with the children; they'd appreciate and enjoy it, especially little Jill, it would be a marvellous opportunity for her to let out some of *her* tremendous paddy! And you'd be helping yourself, too!'

'That *is* a good idea, but do you really think I could "let go" with the children there?'

'Of course you could! It's just what you need to do. You don't *give* yourself to them enough; you'd be surprised at the response if you did! Well, you think about it anyway—and do give it a try—but, most important of all, spend some quiet time at the beginning of the day if possible, filling your mind with *positive* symbols, and feeding the fire with some of those negative thoughts. And remember that you are *never* alone, for I am here. Remember too that I shall *never really* get angry with you, for I accept you for what you are, but it's my task to help you to use and build on those foundations—however shallow and insecure some of them may be at present—and *you* must learn to do the same things: to accept, to use, to build, and above all to forgive.'

The following day (after another octopus nightmare):

'Thank you, Gildas, for the wonderful advice you gave me. Today was so different. I was conscious of struggling with inner problems, but at the same time I had so much energy and determination, and a more placid outlook on life, accepting everything somehow instead of trying to organize things that just won't be organized. I'm sure it was the few moments' quiet positive thinking in the morning. It's worth getting up a few minutes earlier for such a reward! But that dreadful nightmare! I still don't seem able to fight the octopus.'

'I don't think you will fight the octopus until you let out some anger. You might even *use* some of the anger to fight the octopus with. There's a great wealth of energy tied up in that, you know. But first you must unravel the first bit, as it were. You will not be able to *use* the anger until you have loosened it a little, and until you know what it is like. A workman cannot use tools which he does not know, or is not used to, and you cannot use this until you recognize its true character. What's the matter, why can't you start? Are you frightened?'

'Yes, I am. Oh, Gildas, I'm so sorry, I always seem to be frightened of something—oh I'm hopeless, why don't you just give me up?'

'My dear child, don't you know that courage is born of fear?

The person who has never known fear has never shown courage. Then, to be frightened is sometimes healthy, at least it shows that you have *some* understanding of what must be done, and that understanding will help you. But remember that fear cannot be conquered by soft words. Don't you remember the scourging in the cave? The scourge is still there, Ruth, and though it would give me great pain to use it again, it is my duty to show you the way. If only you could make a start we should have something to work on, but only you can decide whether we progress or not. Tell me about the fear. Is it very bad?'

'Yes it is. It paralyses me. It makes me tense. If only I could relax, all the anger would come pouring out, I know, but it is as if I were squashed in a vice. Now talking about it makes me feel dreadful. The tension is so great I could scream.'

'It might be a good idea if you did scream. But take your mind away from it now for a while. Try to absorb yourself in something wholly in the outer world. Try to relax and we will talk again tomorrow.'

That night I had the colour nightmare, and the following night the octopus nightmare.

'Ruth, why didn't you come and talk to me yesterday?'

'I couldn't. I couldn't sit still long enough.'

'But you know you have no need to sit still in order to have a few minutes in the inner world. You could have gone for a walk, or talked to me over tea, or whilst you washed up, or cycled home from school.'

'I know. It wasn't only that I couldn't sit still, it was a general inability to concentrate, an "unquietness of mind". I find it very difficult to talk then, you know.'

'Yes, I know. Yet even now you're not very calm, you're still so tense. What about the positive thinking and the calm attitude you found? Until I mentioned the scourge to you the night before last, you had been so calm, so "deeply strong" all day.'

'I know, this is a dreadful mixture. The meditation in the morning helps enormously and I have been better with the children, had more energy and have been the gentle, calm and yet vivacious "mother" that they expect me to be. We've got through an enormous amount of really creative work these last three days. It is only when talking to you, or when I am alone, that I feel so restless.'

'Yes, I thought so. You are happy so long as you can bury the thought of what you *must* face eventually, but when you begin to think about it, you close up, gripped by this paralysing fear. Now, let's talk about it sensibly and with relaxation. No, don't curl yourself up and chew your fingers; stretch out, get on the bed if it helps, and think yourself calm, bit by bit; force yourself to relax.'

I got on to the bed and bit by bit forced my body, at least, into relaxation. Gildas stood at the end of the bed, looking a trifle anxious. Then he sat down on the bed beside me.

'That's much better. Now think of the positive symbols; draw strength from the Deep Centre. You won't be able to attempt what I have in mind without it.'

In a very short while I had become calm and 'deeply strong' once more, but Gildas still looked anxious and grave.

'I said before that I didn't think you could fight the octopus without first getting some of your anger free in order to use it. But now I think you will be less frightened of the anger if you *can* manage to kill the octopus first. You are using an enormous amount of energy to repress your anger, and you really need it for the battle with the octopus, but if you can hold on to the Deep Centre and the jewel, although it will not be easy, I think you will be able to do it, then the way should be *really* free for the anger. I want you now to fight the octopus, to free yourself from the prison of its tentacles, to kill it, once and for all. Take the jewel with you, it will help you.'

Using active imagination, once more I picked up the angel's sword and the jewel and set out to meet the octopus. A long and fearful battle ensued. At first I found it difficult to find the octopus. I seemed to be sinking, sinking down to the bottom of the sea. Suddenly and without warning, I was almost choked by a revolting tentacle round my neck, and was taken immediately into the semi-freedom within the tentacles of the octopus—but far too near its beady eyes. Brandishing the sword, I cut off a tentacle, but immediately another grew and gripped me in a breath-taking grip. I cut this off, too, and began striking here and there in order to escape the grip of the tentacles, but I had little energy or enthusiasm for the fight and I was soon exhausted. As I gradually ceased to strike with the sword, so the tentacles left me once more in semi-freedom, but always as if in a cage. I was about to cast away the angel's sword, when I felt my foot against a rock. Suddenly I was filled with new vitality. I lifted the sword with a fresh determination, and struck out to right and left. I cut off tentacles, but always fresh ones appeared. I battled for ages, but I was tireless, calm and strong, awaiting the opportunity to escape; suddenly I saw it, the octopus was tiring and seemed to have little control now over its flailing tentacles. Two or three became twisted together and left a gap. As the ugly creature tried to untangle itself, I swam free and up until I was above the octopus, looking down. The angel appeared beside me. 'The jewel,' he said in urgency, 'before it can fully recover. Throw it at the creature.' This I did, or rather dropped it on top of it through the water. Suddenly there was a beautiful flash of light from the jewel, but the octopus was blinded and, as the jewel hit one of its tentacles, it crumpled, helpless and lifeless, and sank with the jewel to the bottom of the sea. I was glad to see the fate of the octopus, but anxious about the jewel.

The angel took my hand. 'Well done,' he said.

'But, Gildas, I have lost the jewel.'

'No, child, you can easily swim down and find it. I will come with you.'

Still holding my hand, Gildas came with me as I swam once more to the bottom of the sea. The octopus was dead and looked very tiny without its tentacles flailing so savagely. Near the octopus was a rock, and beside it the angel's sword and the jewel. Suddenly my attention was drawn to something else, one of the cut-off tentacles of the octopus, but it was ugly no longer, it had turned to gold. I picked it up; it was taller than I, like a golden staff. The angel smiled. 'Keep it,' he said, and misquoted the lines of one of my favourite hymns: 'With it you may "smite the living fountains from the rocks upon your Way". It is yet another positive symbol to help you in your journey to the Light.'

CHAPTER 5

Flaming Fury, the Children, Transformation and the Birth of Astra

March to September 1959

Flaming Fury

The octopus nightmare never returned, but now almost every night the colour nightmare was repeated. Sometimes in dreams I was scourged by the angel. One evening, when I tried to talk to him, Gildas suggested that I should spend the time 'seeking strength' which I did, holding before me the positive symbols, now including the golden staff.

In an inner experience I set out from an island to the mainland on a flimsy raft. There was a storm and the raft was too heavily loaded. I threw things overboard in desperation. At last the storm abated and I realized that all that was left on the raft was a yellow jewel, the snake curled round a rock, a golden flower, a golden staff, and a sword. Suddenly the angel appeared and hoisted a sail, and we landed safely on the mainland.

Scourging and colour nightmares continued. Four days later:

'Ruth, you have been deliberately avoiding a conversation with me. Why?'

'Because I'm frightened of you.'

'You must never be afraid of me. Be afraid of what I might ask you to do if you like, but not afraid of *me*. You have no need to fear me, for I have told you I accept everything you do and

81

everything you are without exception, but always I must try to guide you towards the Light.'

'Oh, for goodness sake forget your wretched sermons for once. All right, it's not you I'm frightened of, it's what I have to face —all this fury; but what *do* you expect me to do when you keep forcing me on, making me meet these horrible situations and fight battles? Do you want me to turn round and say I love you and because I do I'll tolerate everything? Do you think I can go on for ever at the pace I've been going for a month now? Am I never to rebel? Must I listen to reason when the logical part of me is so weary that it won't work any more? The human flesh is frail, Gildas, and really sometimes I could get *so* angry with you, especially just lately. I *do* love you, you know, and without you I am, utterly and hopelessly lost, so please be patient with me when I cannot go as quickly as you would wish.'

'Congratulations, my dear! You came as near then to a flaming fury as you have come for a long time. Why on earth didn't you really let go? Of course you can rebel if you want to. If only you will let it happen, you can be as free as you can be, you can be *you*, wholly and completely. What does it matter what other people say or think so long as you observe certain basic rules of courtesy, tolerance and consideration for others without which social life would be impossible? But you don't need to expand these rules until they form a kind of moral fence around you, allowing you only a restricted area in which to move, even preventing you from making satisfactory human relationships. Letting out your anger will be a good step towards this freedom —and by all means let it out on me if you like; it can't harm me for I know its nature already. There is nothing there for which I am unprepared. But whatever way you choose *please* give it *some* expression soon.'

'Oh, Gildas, there is still a dreadful block, stopping its free passage. I realize that it is a form of conceit to think that my anger can do any *real* harm to anyone. I am prepared for the fact that I shall probably look an utter fool when eventually I do give vent to my feelings. I accept the fact that I am as other people, that I have a temper and I no longer want to repress it in order to feel superior—yet still there is something in the way.'

'What is it, do you know?'

'Yes, I think it's just a matter of habit. I've grown so used to never showing a bad temper or being visibly annoyed that now I do it almost naturally, and before I discover how cross I really am about a thing, the really violent feelings have gone.'

After this talk, and for the first night for ages, I had no dreams! Then the colour nightmares returned. I made some attempts to let out anger, but after three weeks had passed I felt I had failed miserably. Gently, the angel said :

'Ruth, will you never learn that I love you? And that because I love you I am willing to help you in *anything*—especially your failures, for surely that is the time when you most need love and understanding?'

'Oh yes, Gildas, it is, but I was so afraid to ask you for help.'

'You have some very mistaken ideas about me, haven't you? I am not the stern parent, you know, who blames you for all your mistakes and faults and failures. I have often told you that I am here to help you no matter *what* you do, but this is something which you are very slow to learn. Perhaps it is because you do not yet understand the full meaning of love. Until you have learned to love someone completely and selflessly you will probably never understand what I mean.'

In a dream we were going along the road to school, the angel and I. We came to a field where there were lots of children. We went into the field and the children asked the angel to tell them a story. He did. Then, after the story they asked us to play with them, and when we finished playing, the children said they had to go home. So we went with them to their house in the woods which was filthily dirty and horrible. They all seemed to be running round eating dry crusts. They had no mother. They all went to bed and made a fearful fuss about it—noise and milling around. Then the angel and I went away.

Soon after, in the outer world I wrote an angry letter to Dr. Swainson. Afterwards I felt much better and that night there was no colour nightmare. Then came a wonderful experience with the children at school. It was a beautiful morning, so I decided to take movement outdoors. On a sudden inspiration I decided to do a dance-drama with percussion. Until the very last minute I had no idea what we were to do a drama *of*, but I gathered the children round me and said that I would tell them a story which we could dance. Suddenly, without conscious preparation or decision, I found myself telling them the story of *The Dream*: the struggle with the snake, the finding of the angel, the arduous journey, the finding of the jewel, the long return to daylight and the woodland. The children were entranced, but what impressed me most was their unquestioning *acceptance* (one might almost say *understanding*) of everything—and they danced with complete absorption—and I danced with them. I think we were all sorry when we eventually had to stop and go inside, but we had been dancing for an hour and had lost all thought of time. Even now I don't understand what prompted me to take this theme, but the experience was one which I am sure I shall always remember.

After I had lost my temper with someone, Gildas was pleased and said, 'Well done.' At this point I talked with him about Dr. Swainson.

'Gildas, it *is* interesting that you never mention Dr. Swainson. Why not?'

'Well, Ruth, there are two reasons. One is in yourself, and I think you realize that really, though you wouldn't admit it to Dr. Swainson. You *have* got a terrific bar against talking about her or mentioning her.

'The other reason why I don't broach the subject is because I don't want you to get the idea that I am a *part* of psychotherapy —that I am inextricably linked with this process of analysis. In some ways, of course, I am, but I have a life outside the analytical experience too. I am with you for ever, your guide, comforter, helper; and I am not limited to one sphere of your life. You have enough doubts about my reality without my always connecting myself with Dr. Swainson—who, in her turn, is connected with an experience which you hardly deign to recognize as realistic although it helps you. Why have you this attitude, do you know?'

'Oh Gildas, I was expecting that one. How I hate being precise and expressing my feelings! I'd much rather leave them in a jumble. Yes, I think I know why. It wouldn't be so bad if I didn't find it so helpful to see Dr. Swainson, but the fact that I do hurts my pride. I like to feel self-sufficient, and I don't welcome the idea that I need help. Going to see Dr. Swainson is a threat to my independence, and yet, contrarily enough, I know she can show me the way to *true* independence. But being rational doesn't help. What do you think of this idea of Dr. Swainson's that she fails me by being the kind of therapist that I can't get angry with?'

'Of course she fails you! She would hardly be human if she didn't. Actually, now you have started on the expression of this "flaming fury" she doesn't *need* any more to be the kind of person you can get angry with—in fact it is probably better that she isn't. During this period you need *someone* with whom you can maintain a stable, sympathetic relationship, because sooner or later you'll probably lose your temper with most people you know! What you needed was something to start you off—and Dr. Swainson gave you that. She did succeed in making you angry and at last you managed to express it. You might have got angry with her before, I think, were it not for the fact that Dr. Swainson is somewhat over-cautious with you. She has rather too much respect for the fact that you tend to be so sensitive; I sometimes get the impression that she is afraid to hurt you. But I am sorry to say that sometimes the *only* way to teach you is to hurt you; you are so stubborn that things really have to go in deep before you recognize them as true. In other words, for you, the joy of release—which comes when one knows and recognizes the truth—is literally not possible without suffering.'

One night, just before going to sleep, I suddenly felt terrified of nothing in particular. I sought the presence of Gildas, but could make no contact with him. I seemed to be cut off from all things. I got up and wandered round my room, still with a great feeling of terror and foreboding. Finally I went into the kitchen and made a hot milk drink and gradually I became calm, but still I could not contact Gildas. I went back to bed where, interspersed with long periods of wakefulness, came a new nightmare. Once again it took place in the prehistoric forest. I was running away from a great danger, for overhead monsters were flying, but they would suddenly drop to the ground and were so heavy that they crushed great areas of growth with them. I had to run and run to escape being crushed too, and always as another monster dropped I just missed being its victim! The terror of this dream was almost indescribable—far worse than the colour nightmare.

Again, I dreamed I was in prison. I kept insisting that I had done nothing wrong, that there was no need to imprison me, that it was all a mistake, but I was left unheeded to lie in misery in a gloomy cell, naked, with only straw to lie on and bread and water to eat.

'Oh, Gildas, I feel utterly wretched.'

'Why, Ruth? I should have thought that you would have felt much better after tonight's outburst.'

'Well, I don't. Oh, it's all very well for you to say "Let this flaming fury out", but *why* must it be let out on *people*? Bad temper causes no end of misery. Just look at tonight's "outburst" as you term it—three other people besides myself thoroughly upset, all because I decided to let my feelings fly, all because I was acting on this wretched maxim "don't bottle things up!"'

Later I found that I had exaggerated the harm I could do; that some people indeed preferred an outburst rather than a strained atmosphere, and as a result became more friendly.

The Children

In the inner world, and *not* this time in a sleep-dream, once more I experienced the walk with Gildas, his telling the children a story, playing with them, and finally going home with them to their filthy house in the forest. This time it was clearer, and I saw that the house where the children lived was *appalling*; it was almost falling down and the filth was ankle-deep. The children were half-naked and half-starved, their bones showing through their skin, but I felt no pity for them, I was only disgusted—they were little better than animals.

Gildas suggested that we should put them to bed and tell them a goodnight story, but I was horrified. 'What,' I screamed, 'stay in this filthy hovel longer than necessary? No fear!' The children heard me, and some of them (there were about twelve altogether) began to cry; one of the bigger ones flung its arms round me and said, 'Oh please don't go, we need a mother, someone to love us and help us, please stay.' I threw the horrid creature from me and, as I did so, Gildas gave me a compassionate but anxious glance; he picked up two of the tiny children and said, 'Well, I'll stay for a while, anyway.' Suddenly I felt shut out and deserted; I turned and ran into the thick forest until I could run no longer. Then utterly exhausted and bewildered, I sat down under a tree and wept.

There Gildas found me, sat beside me, and took my hand.

'What are you running away from?'

'Oh, those children, those children, take me away from them, Gildas—right away—they're horrible, too horrible for words.'

'Ruth, I can't take you away from them, they are part of you —and I'm afraid you must face them.'

'But they're so disgusting. You are sympathetic towards them, but how you can be I don't know. They have no refinements at all.'

'That is because their mother has never taken an interest in them. She deserted them and refuses to come back, but they need her so badly, and they are nice children really.'

'Well, why on earth don't you find the mother and *make* her come back?'

'I have found her, Ruth, she is right here beside me—she is you. Are you going to set about the task of "refining" your family?'

'No, Gildas, never. I don't own children like that; you're trying to make me *think* that I do. I don't *know* how to be a mother. I don't know how to love.'

'No, but the children know what they want and they can certainly teach you how to love, and I am here to guide you and encourage you. It isn't easy, but you must try.'

I was suddenly angry. 'Oh, GO AWAY! GO AWAY! Leave me alone! Go and look after the beastly children yourself. Don't ever come near me again, I HATE YOU and I wish I'd never met you!'

'Well, this is one time when I refuse to go away, Ruth. The children certainly need to be looked after, but *you* need a lot of love too; no harm will come to the children if we leave them for a few more days; they have been alone for long enough. I will stay here with you until you feel able to contact your inner sources of strength and face the task in front of you. I love you and I hate to see you so upset, but it will all come right in the end. Meanwhile you may tell me anything. The more you tell me about your feelings, the more I can help you. But if you don't want to talk, that's all right.'

'Gildas, I'm so sorry—you're such a comfort; I *will* try to understand.'

'I know, but don't rush, this is rather a shock, isn't it? Rest, and get over that first, then we will have another look at the children.'

(This experience was repeated in a sleep-dream.)

I worked on the experience, using free writing, but more than three weeks later I felt just as bad.

'Gildas, please go away. I'm not meaning to be unco-operative, but I feel so wretched and miserable, I just can't bear to have anyone near me, even you. All the time you're with me I feel you want me to go on, to face those dreadful children—and I can't, I really can't.'

'Ruth, how unreasonable you think I am. Of course I don't expect you to go on, feeling as you do at the moment. I am sorry that the way is so hard and your unhappiness so great, and I want to help you. Tell me about all this misery, you will feel better if you talk about it.'

'It's like an agonizing pain, Gildas. The octopus is dead—but only at tremendous cost. The wounds are so deep they still hurt, and I feel as though they will never heal.' We continued with a deeper talk, and I was able to do more writing, as a kind of psychological autobiography. Eleven days later :

'Gildas, tell me about your love for me, this love which you say can heal so surely. It is not a physical love, is it?'

'No, dear, it is not. It is a spiritual love of great power. When you learn to love too, to lose yourself wholly in me, then together we shall attain to great heights of spiritual joy and experience—far beyond anything you can yet imagine. Love is the greatest power on earth, and though my love for you, alone, might achieve great things, when you too can love then whole new fields of spiritual experience will be open to you.

'I have told you that the creative power of love can heal—and so my love will heal you. This is what psychotherapy is, too: the creative power of love used to heal human beings.'

'Gildas, I *do* love you—but I suppose it's not enough yet?'

'No. You have to experience selfless love; but one day when you are not thinking about it particularly it will come, and you will find that, perhaps even against your own inclination, you want to do something for someone else because *they* want it and you love them. But don't worry about it. Your first step in learning such love must be to care for the children. I hope you haven't forgotten them?'

'How could I, when I dream of them? But I cannot do it yet —not yet.'

(Very gentle but very firm): 'Ruth, you cannot put it off for ever. It is time you emerged from this period of inactivity and gathered your strength to go forward.'

'Gildas, I *won't*—you can't *make* me—I can think of nothing more revolting than learning to love these ghastly children. They've survived so long, they'll probably go on surviving.'

'You can be very cruel, Ruth, can't you? Yes, you're quite right, the children will probably survive, but you know what some of the effects that lack of affection and care can have on children, and these children are no exception. Unless you care for them before it is too late, your task will become well-nigh impossible. No, Ruth, I can't *make* you do anything, but because I love you I must do all in my power to teach you the right thing to do. I have had to take up the scourge before, must I do so again?'

'You can please yourself, but whatever you do it will make no difference.'

In dreams again I was scourged. After nearly a week:

'Gildas, I know you are angry with me, but please help me.'

'Ruth, I am not angry with you, only sad, and of course I am ready to help you; what is the matter?'

'I feel so wretched. It is as if suddenly everything had overwhelmed me and I feel helpless. Oh, Gildas, what is life for? We go rushing round in circles, busy about doing nothing, never really accomplishing anything except noise and unhappiness and unquietness of spirit. At times it is so unbearable I wonder whether it is all an illusion and whether we are all sinful spirits condemned to eternal torment. There is no peace, Gildas, except in the realms of the spirit. Materialism is ugly and modern values are out of balance. The more "civilized" we become, it seems, the further behind us we leave all hopes of true happiness. Sometimes I feel that the only way to be free without committing the sin of breaking the thread of life would be to possess nothing and to live the solitary life of a contemplative cut off from all that is worldly. Oh, what's the use, I *can't* put it all into words, but at times like this it's unbearable.'

'Ruth, many of these questions you must find an answer to yourself—an answer which will probably not always seem satisfactory to you, which will have to be changed, but nevertheless which must always be given from yourself in order to be satisfactory. Do you remember the picture I once showed you of the sowing and reaping of grain, and told you how that is symbolic of the coming of truth to the human mind? You have a reverence for life, Ruth, for you speak of "the sin of breaking the thread of life", and that reverence is something to build on. I am sorry that you are so unhappy and perplexed, but times like this come to everyone and I am here to lead you in the Light. And, Ruth, remember the beautiful experience at the Tower—then all things were One, "woven together in a kind of spiritual unity".'

Again in dreams I was scourged by the angel. Five days later :

'Ruth, you cannot go on like this for ever. WHEN are you going to decide to face up to the task of dealing with those children? If only you would make a start I'm sure you wouldn't find it as bad as you imagine it to be.'

'Yes, Gildas, I'm sorry, I'm behaving dreadfully over this but I'm terrified—and even your scourge is preferable to this ordeal. However, you're right, I know, and I *must* try. Help me, Gildas, I know I have the strength of the Deep Centre and all those wonderful symbols, but the strength I get from these is used to its fullest when you advise and guide me—and love me.'

'Of course I will help you, and of course I love you. Do you remember that one symbol for the Deep Centre is the rock? And do you remember the golden staff? Upright on the rock it is a symbol of great power, and if you can visualize it clearly and not lose sight of it, you will not fail in strength. Remember that you are to "smite the living fountains from the rocks along your way".'

'Gildas, before we go any further, what about Dr. Swainson's idea that a more positive, tolerant, accepting attitude would make the children seem less scruffy and unruly? Is it a good idea, as she says, to approach this in a somewhat roundabout manner?'

'Yes, I think it is, for it will lessen your fear. It is your own unconscious attitudes which make the children appear so scruffy and unruly, and though we shall have to deal with that attitude later, if you can temporarily get rid of it, it may make things easier. Think back, as Dr. Swainson suggested, to the sunny morning on Saturday, and the atmosphere of trust and understanding, acceptance and love, and carry it over if you can into creative imagination (for that is the best way to start on this, at least). Don't go rushing into this, but just think over all I have said and all that Dr. Swainson has said; relax if you can, and let it happen. I will be with you.'

Transformation

During the next ten days the following experiences took place; they were a jumble of 'creative imagination', a sleep-dream, and actual inner experience; in looking back afterwards I was not sure which was which.

First, I visualised the 'symbol of power', setting it firmly above and before me. As I concentrated, I was given marvellous proof of the strength of the Deep Centre, for under the rock I saw the water of the spirit, and round the whole symbol appeared the most beautiful rainbow made up of the six colours which I had seen in the cave: red, green, blue, yellow, white, and purple.

I tried hard to get a new, positive attitude towards the children. Once again I saw the wood. Everything was hazy and muddled, the angel was with me but suddenly all went dark, I could not see, but Gildas took my hand and led me on. Many times I stumbled, but Gildas held me firmly and when I would

have stopped, to wait for the darkness to clear, he led me onwards in silent determination. Suddenly it began to rain, in
torrents. But still Gildas would not stop. I began to shiver violently
with cold and fear, but Gildas threw his cloak about my shoulders
—still without speaking—and as he did so I saw clearly above
and before me the symbol of the golden staff on the rock, the
symbol of power and strength which I had almost forgotten; as I
concentrated on it the rain stopped.

Still it was dark, and now the wind came so strongly that I
could hardly stand against it, but Gildas held me firmly close to
him; the symbol was ever before me and we kept on and on.

Now it began to get light again; the wind stopped and the
sun came out. Gildas relaxed his grip on me and we walked
serenely through the beautiful forest—on towards the house
where the children would be.

Now I saw the house, in the sunlight, but it no longer seemed
ancient and tumbledown—in fact it was rather a charming
woodland cottage. It was no longer misty and I could see the
thatched roof and roses round the door. It was neglected, though;
the garden was full of weeds, the roses untrained, the cottage
needed painting and the windows needed cleaning, but there
was none of the filth which had so horrified me before. This was
merely neglect which could soon be remedied.

Inside the cottage the children were waiting as though expecting something to happen. They had tried to look their best,
but they, too, were neglected, their clothes were torn, their hair
was untidy, they were thin and underfed, but again they were
not dirty as before, nor unruly.

Suddenly I noticed there were not so many children as I had
thought: there were only five instead of twelve. I turned to
Gildas.

'Where are the other children?'

'There are no other children, Ruth. I told you your task was
less difficult than you imagined. You were so horrified and panic-
stricken before that you literally "saw things"; there appeared to
be far more children than there really were. But now you are
facing things more calmly they have come back into their right
perspective. I did not tell you before for I thought it better for

you to find out for yourself. Now, my child, you must get to know your family. There is much to do for them and they need a lot of love, but they will also give you a lot of love. Don't be afraid, for I am here to help you.'

Reconstruction

[Most of the narrative so far has been taken from a diary, the transformation occurring at the end of June 1959. During the summer vacation, however, I took a rest from daily recording, and the following account was written in early September. All the 'work' described was direct experience in the inner world; there was no active imagination, and while the work continued I dreamed very little. The experience did not, as so often it had done before, carry over into dreams.]

To attempt to describe the joy which I now experience in the inner world would be an impossible task. Throughout the summer vacation, with the loving help of Gildas, I have worked hard with the children. Strangely enough, while the work lasted I found that I could not write about it, but Gildas told me that the time would come when I should be able to do so. That time is here now, but some memories of the work are dim and lacking in detail. I asked Gildas about this too, and he was able to reassure me.

'It is only natural, my dear, that your memories should be dim, for you will remember that some of the work was painful for you in the extreme, and repulsive too. You have been brave, my child, and what you have achieved in the innermost parts of yourself will be with you for ever. It is enough that you should have suffered, and it is not necessary for you to remember every detail of your suffering. Also, some of this work has taken place at that deep unconscious level where you are aware only of a change in your approach, but only dimly—if at all—aware of the process of arriving at the change.'

The most hazy part of this work concerns the character of the children. They seem to have left little impression on me at a conscious level, as individuals, and yet it seems that at the deeper level I knew them well; but I never gave them names nor learned any that they may already have had.

93

First of all Gildas said the most important thing was for me to learn to give love to the children and to receive their love. On our arrival at the cottage the children were waiting, and after some wary glances at me welcomed Gildas with open arms. He played with them, fondled them, kissed them, and they obviously adored him. I made a terrific effort to overcome my feelings and do likewise, but I could not. I really *hated* those children. Suddenly a rather grimy little boy rushed at me. 'You've come to be our mother, and I love you,' he said, flinging his arms around my neck. I was horrified and threw him away from me with some force, so that he fell heavily and lay on the floor, bewildered and whimpering at this refusal of his love—all he had to offer. I ran to another room—the kitchen—and wept bitterly. Presently Gildas came. He uttered no rebuke, but put his arms round me until my weeping had stopped. I looked up at him then and said, 'It's no use, Gildas, I can't do it, I've tried and I can't.' Then, with a very tender look, Gildas said, 'I know you can't do it for yourself, but don't you think you could do it for me?' Suddenly all my love for Gildas was there, and I knew that I would do anything for him, so I nodded my head. He understood immediately. 'I told the children that you were tired and that they must treat you gently,' he said, 'but will you come to them now?' Without hesitation I went with Gildas to the children, picked up the child who had claimed me as mother, and told them all that I was sorry for the incident, but that I had indeed come to be their mother, that I would look after them and love them, and never leave them again.

This 'opening incident' I remember clearly, but next we set to work to clean and repair and dig and cultivate—and to tame the children. I spent much time in the inner world, but remember no details of this period, except that gradually I came to love the children and we were a happy family and had many happy times together. Always Gildas was there and, as I learned to love the children, so my love for him grew, and I remembered what he had once said to me, 'One day . . . you will find that, perhaps against your own inclination, you want to do something for someone because *they* want it and *you* love them.'

All this must have taken three or four weeks. Then one day Gildas came to me looking very grave, and he spoke very gently to me, as we stood at the door of our cottage, which now looked really charming after all our work.

'You have heard the story of the House built on Sand, and the House built on Rock, haven't you?"

'Yes, of course.'

'Well, my dear, I'm sorry to say that this house is built on sand—and we must take it to pieces, brick by brick, and build it again on the rock at the other side of the wood."

This was a terrible task, but I soon realized that it must be done. The pain of taking the house to pieces and rebuilding it was almost physical—it seemed as if it were I who was being torn apart. But we toiled night and day until our task was completed, the children helping with a will.

The Birth of Astra

Soon after the House on the Rock was finished, I asked Gildas and the children if I might go away alone for awhile, and they agreed I should do so if I really wanted to.

I told no one where I was going, or why, but I wished to be alone in a secret glade in the forest, that there I might give birth to my baby, hide it and visit it in secret. No one knew, I thought, or would understand this wonderful thing which was to happen to me.

No sooner had I reached the glade, however, than I wished that Gildas were with me, but I was hot and tired and fell into a troubled sleep. When I awoke, Gildas was beside me. 'I knew you wanted me,' he said, 'so I came. Why do you try to hide things from me, when I know you through and through?'

'Gildas,' I said, 'I came to give birth to a baby.'

'I know, it is our baby, to be born because you have learned to love. Why do you want to hide it and keep it in secret? Am I such an ogre to you that you must hide our child from me?'

'No, Gildas, you know that I regretted it as soon as I arrived here alone. I just had to be sure that you would understand.'

'My dear, you always have my understanding, you haven't any need to ask for it.'

'Gildas, stay with me until the child is born.'

And so Gildas was with me when our beautiful baby girl was born. I asked him to name her, and he called her Astra. She was a beautiful child, and Gildas wrapped her in a lovely shawl which he had brought with him (I had no such forethought), then gently he put her at my breast. 'You must nourish and cherish her,' he said, 'and she will grow in beauty, for she is your newborn love.'

The Divine Mother

For a while I was happy with Astra and the other children (who adored the new baby) but then I grew anxious and troubled. Gildas took me with him, alone, for a walk.

'What is troubling you, Ruth?'

'Gildas, how can I really be a good mother to Astra and the others when I have no inner image of proper motherhood to call on? I have grown to love them so much, I should hate to fail them in any way.'

For answer, Gildas bade me continue our walk, which we did until we came to the foot of some mountains. Soon, among the rocks we saw a rushing river, and stopped on its banks near a cave. I looked at the cave and had a sudden fear that it might contain the octopus, but Gildas said, 'Don't be afraid; you have slain the octopus—but look at the water over there.'

I looked and saw—slowly rising from the water—a vision of a very beautiful woman, dressed in flowing robes. Her face showed maturity, suffering, compassion, and great love. And when she spoke, her voice was very beautiful (I actually heard it): 'Every human being has a divine mother, my dear, for it is I; I am the mother of all, and there is of me in every woman, if only she will allow herself to discover it.' And as suddenly as it had come, the vision was gone, but I remembered some words I had once heard : 'God is Mother as well as Father.'

CHAPTER 6

The True Return and Marriage in the Inner World

September 1959 to April 1960

One night, when on holiday, I was sitting in the garden of the hotel, watching the lights of the village on the opposite bank of the estuary shining in the water. It was a beautiful scene and I was quite alone. Then Gildas was with me in the inner world, holding out his hands to me. As I took his hands I had the odd experience of watching myself. Where before I had been sitting in the darkest part of the garden, there seemed to be a brilliant light, and in the distance I could see golden mountains. As Gildas held my hands he seemed to float upwards and to take with him a part of me—a blue shadow—and away he floated over the peaks of the golden mountains and out of sight. Suddenly all was dark again, and as before I sat looking at the lights on the water. Yet I felt that a part of me had gone; I did not feel 'whole' but I was at peace. Presently Gildas returned and with him brought the blue shadow. I was 'whole' again and filled with a wonderful sense of well-being impossible to describe. Somewhere in the golden mountains a part of me had undergone a transformation. I had this experience several times since, usually when I was tired or anxious.

The True Return

I was back at work and living much more in the outer world when one day I asked Gildas if marriage were to be part of my life.

97

'In all things, Ruth, men have free will, and it is not given that I should foretell the events of your life, except in the most general of terms. One thing is certain, you have worked for and have been given a great deal, and the kinds of experiences which you have had are sent into the world to lighten it, and, because you have had these experiences, whatever path of life you choose to follow you will—unless you turn from the Light—have much to give to the world.

'I have told you before that there is a great work for you to do—a work that would require you to dedicate yourself whole-heartedly to it. But it is you who must choose; if you pass through the doors which at various points of your life will be opened to you, then you will find the work. Yet not to choose this path is no sin and perhaps if the opportunity of marriage comes your way, you will take it. What you must remember is that marriage, too, can be a grand and creative work, bringing light to the world.

'Most important of all, Ruth, you have a priceless gift; you have learned some of the secrets of life at its deepest level, and because of this you have a great responsibility. You must not live for yourself alone, but for others, that they too may learn of these things. This will take great courage, but you have that courage, and you know that you are never alone and that there are sources of strength far, far greater than that to be found in the individual ego. You will need, too, a deep humility, but that you will find will grow in you with advancing years. Above all, relax and learn to live as much as possible in the present and be assured that, in the familiar phrase, "the future will take care of itself".'

Five weeks later :

'What is the matter, Ruth, you look very perplexed?'

'Only superficially so, Gildas; really I am very serene and happy, you know that. It's just—well, there is so little happening in the inner world now. I know that you have told me that you will always be with me, and we have Astra and the children too, but though in the inner world I have suffered much, I have also learned the greatest joy and I should hate to feel that all the activity there had ceased for ever—and was lost.'

'My poor child, what ideas you get hold of sometimes! The inner world will never be lost; every time you come to me, every time you care for Astra or the children, you enter into the inner world and live there a life which is rich and full. But don't forget, Ruth, that for almost two years you have lived and worked and experienced a great deal in the inner world, all of which is mentally exhausting. You may not realize it—for now you are living from the inexhaustible strength of the Deep Centre —but you are, mentally, very tired. Throughout your struggles, your foot was not always on the Rock! Also I told you once that the coming of truth to the human mind was like a series of harvests. My dear, you have reaped a glorious harvest and your cup is full; now the earth must remain fallow for a while in preparation for harvests to come.

'So, Ruth, for the time being you may look forward to a period of comparative peace in the inner world, but you must never think that you have lost your inner life; once found it is rarely lost; and you can certainly never lose all that you have achieved.

'Yet do not let me give you the impression that your work is at an end. Far from it, my child; this period of relative inactivity in the inner world marks the True Return.

'You will never be really "of the earth, earthy", it is not in your nature, but you must strive to find genuine pleasure in the ordinary business of living. Persevere in human relationships, and take to the world the Light which you have been privileged to see. You must also remain humble and realize that the world may also have much to give you.

'Ask Dr. Swainson to help you with this True Return. She, having trodden the way before, can do so far better than I. But go gently, don't rush, and rest in the peace and serenity of the Deep Centre.'

Six weeks later, in the silence and tranquillity of a Quaker Meeting, I had an inner experience in which I was reunited with Gildas.

I was in a deep pit, dirty, naked, and in despair. I could not climb out for the sides were sheer and slippery. I could only gaze at the patch of light, so far away, which marked the top of the pit. Then I noticed that above the pit there seemed to be a white mountain, similar to the one which I saw at the beginning of the inner journey, when I first met Gildas. My despair deepened, there seemed no way out of the pit; I was alone and knew that somewhere my child Astra was without her mother, but I couldn't remember where I had left her. Suddenly the light above me was intensified and, looking up, I was almost dazzled by its brilliance. When I became more accustomed to it I could see the white mountain very clearly, and on its peak stood Gildas, holding Astra in his arms. I was overjoyed to see them and made desperate and vain attempts to climb out of the pit. Finally, exhausted, I looked up again, and saw that Gildas was also holding what appeared to be a ladder made from shining golden cord, and to my joy he let this ladder down until it reached me. I was weak and tired, but knew that I must reach Gildas in my own strength by climbing the ladder unaided. The journey seemed unending and each step was agony—but at last I stood on the mountain peak, reunited with Gildas and Astra. Now, as at our first meeting, I was led to a spring where I washed and put on a clean white robe; then Gildas tied a golden chain round my waist, and on the end of the chain hung the jewel. 'There,' said Gildas, 'now you will not forget to take the jewel wherever you go.' I smiled and held out my arms for Astra, and gently Gildas gave her to me again, then we sat down together without speaking, content to be reunited.

The first joys of reunion over, I was full of questions about the reasons for our parting, but Gildas gave me a look of infinite compassion, and something in his face told me that he, too, had suffered. I knelt before him and he put gentle hands on my head.

'My dear child, how you have suffered—and so unnecessarily too. It need not have been like this, but you are still so rebellious. I try to mould you like wax, and yet you are sometimes stiff and unresponsive. I told you that you must try to live in the outer world, knowing that great demands would be made on you there at this time of the year. I warned you to expect a lull in the activity in the inner world. But you didn't accept this, you

were angry with me, and so lost contact with me, for I cannot
come to you unless you are ready to receive me.'

'But Gildas, Dr. Swainson showed me how stupid my anger
was; why couldn't I make contact with you after that?'

'This was a time of testing, Ruth, and I could not come to you.
You had to live through this period without my guidance, relying solely on the Deep Centre and your own strength. I should
have explained all this if only your anger had not prevented me
from coming to you just before the time of testing. Things might
still have been difficult for you, the test would still have been
harsh, but much of the anguish you have suffered need never
have been.'

'Gildas, I am sorry; you have suffered too, haven't you?'

'Yes, Ruth, but only because my love for you is such that
your suffering is also mine—and remember your joy is mine,
too.'

'Then I have failed the test through being so unresponsive?'

'No, my dear, *of course* you haven't failed! You have done
and are doing all that is required of you. Can you feel the
pleasure in all that you are achieving, in the way in which you
are giving yourself to the children at school, and helping to
create for them the wonder of Christmastide? This would be
justifiable pride, you know. Do try to feel it, Ruth, for it will
help you to begin to value the life of the outer world.

'Now, my child, the test continues, and though I shall not go
away in the absolute sense, as I did before, you must keep set
times for coming to me, and devote the rest of your energies
to this business of living. The most hectic part of the term is still
to come—but I am here, and the jewel is at your waist. The
second part of the test will not be as painful as the first.'

Two days later, in bed :

'Gildas, after all you have said to me I feel unclean—as if I
need to be purified.'

'I know, Ruth, but sleep now, for your body needs refreshment too, and perhaps your purification will come as you sleep,
if you are ready for it.'

I went to sleep and dreamed that I was wandering in a wild
and desolate place, rocky and sandy with no vegetation. Suddenly

the sand and the rocks began to burn, and I was walking through fire, but felt no pain, only a cleansing. After the fire came wind, followed by rain—and when I woke I no longer felt the need for purification. I was clean once more and could 'start again', at peace with myself.

Preparation for Marriage

'Gildas, am I wrong to feel as I do about becoming "a frustrated spinster"?'

'No, Ruth, of course not, didn't Dr. Swainson tell you it was only natural? And so it is. I have told you before that you are free to choose your own way of life, and if you feel marriage cannot be part of life for you then you must take steps to deal with the fears and emotions that are aroused by such a decision. Dr. Swainson will help you better than I—she is a woman! Also, your time of testing in the outer world is not yet over, and I have told you that I cannot often be with you or help you.

'One thing, though, when this time is over, we have some work to do on our relationship which will probably help you to feel better. You have tended to regard me as a "father", and in many ways I have so far accepted and even encouraged this attitude, as it seemed to be the way in which I could best help you and give you strength throughout the intense inner activity. Yet soon you must come to accept me as a lover, a husband, the father of your child—not in any physical sense but in a glorious spiritual union which will bring us both great joy. This is something which we will work on, and which you must learn to accept; our relationship must be more mature on your side, a relationship between man and woman, not father and child. When we establish this, as I have said, there will be great joy, and some of your fears will be allayed, for you will have this "inner fulfilment"—you have it now but don't feel it in its deepest sense because you are still far too ready to play the role of the dependent child. It is best though, that first you should talk with Dr. Swainson and try to resolve this problem from the outside; the inner side must wait awhile and will probably come more easily once you have faced the outer.

'You once asked if you relied on me too much, and this is

your answer. It is not that you rely on me too much, it is the way in which you do so. You will find this re-examination of our relationship difficult, but you may be assured that I shall not ask anything of you until you are ready.'

In a dream I was walking with Gildas in a dark tunnel. All we could see was a faint glimmering of light in the distance, and towards this we went. Suddenly the light disappeared, all was dark, so dark that every time I took a step I stumbled. Although both Gildas and I were dressed in white I couldn't see either his clothes or my own. I could only feel Astra in my arms. I became panic-stricken and screamed, but in the dark Gildas took my hand and said, 'Sit down and remain still; one must only move forward when the way is clear, the light shining.'

Again, in a dream I was climbing up a mountain towards Gildas who stood at the top. The way was very hard, and I had Astra in my arms so that I could not pull myself up the steep path with the help of my hands. I progressed slowly and pain-fully until I came to a part of the mountain which was even steeper, and where the path was covered with loose stones. My feet began to slip and I could see no foothold at all. I was frantic, until I heard Gildas say calmly, 'Stay where you are, I will come to you. When there are no footholds in sight it is best to rest for awhile and later to look again.'

I had been restless, unhappy and discontented, wondering whether to start looking for another teaching post, unable to come to terms either with life or with myself. Several times Gildas had said to me, 'When you are ready you will *know*.' I seemed un-able to accept this or to achieve any quietude of mind.

For a few days I had been wandering with Gildas in the inner world in a wild and desolate place—but now he led me from the pathway, up a mountain and then through a rocky mountain pass into a valley, sheltered and cut off from the world. Here all was tranquil and unspoiled, and of indescribable beauty. We sat in silence, and once again I experienced that wonderful feel-ing that all things are One, unified in God. Later, when we left the valley, I was at peace, all things seemed to have come into perspective, and I knew the truth of what Gildas had said before : 'When you are ready, you will *know*'.

In January, in a dream I was walking with Gildas across fields of ice and snow; all was white and pure, but there was no sign of vegetation. Soon darkness began to fall, and Gildas said that we must sleep, so we lay down on the ice and I slept almost immediately. I awoke to find myself naked and covered with writhing snakes. At first I was horrified, but then became alive to the pleasant sensation caused by the movement of the snakes over my body and soon I slept again, untroubled.

In February, I was writing a letter when Gildas was present with me in a very vivid way, and the room seemed to be filled with his love and light. I went into the inner world where I was still walking through a wilderness of ice and snow. Suddenly we saw a shape, totally frozen and encased in thick ice. I felt that this thing, whatever it might be, was important, but obviously the task of removing the ice was an impossible one. Gildas told me to kneel with him on the ice, near the shape, and to pray for light. This we did, and our prayers were most marvellously answered. Suddenly there was a great light and warmth all around us, and even as we watched the ice began to melt—and soon revealed a glorious golden fountain, playing water coloured in all colours of the rainbow. But it was the shape of the fountain which struck me, with its bowl and its spike; it was a combination of male and female symbols.

In March I had a recurring nightmare in which I was being chased across thin ice by hundreds of small black demons carrying flaming torches. I ran until I was exhausted, and when I stopped for breath the demons gathered round and melted the ice from under my feet. As I slipped down into the blackest depths, I woke up terrified.

After a few days the nightmare changed. This time, as I slipped into the black water when the ice melted, I suddenly stopped being afraid and floated on down and down—accepting the blackness and at peace with myself. The sinking seemed to go on for a very long time, until suddenly there was light, and I found myself standing in a beautiful sunny clearing in a forest, with Gildas. In front of us was a pond of clearest blue water. I felt very heavy, and looking down saw that I was dressed in filthy rags, covered in mud and slime. I felt heavy because there were stones and weights tied to the repulsive rags.

Gildas told me to take off the rags, but my fear returned. I tried to run away, but was too weighted down to do so. Very gently Gildas took my hands. 'Take them off, my beloved; the suffering will soon be over.' I knelt at his feet and wept bitterly, but Gildas with a look of resolution began to strip off the rags. I screamed, for the pain was almost unbearable, as if my very skin was being torn from my bones. At last the agony was over. Gildas tossed the rags into the blue pond which, for a moment, became muddy and turbulent, but was soon clear and still once more. Joyfully I stood up, hand in hand with Gildas, to find that I was dressed in a flowing robe of soft green linen—and I felt light, lighter than air. Tenderly Gildas took me into his arms and kissed me—and I awoke with a feeling of great peace in my mind.

In early April I dreamed that I was trapped with some pre-historic monsters in a horrid muddy forest. The monsters were enormous and flat and utterly repulsive. I was very frightened, but slowly the mud changed until it became water, and the monsters nothing but pieces of rubbish and driftwood floating on the surface, and I was drifting on the water in a boat. The water was dirty and unpleasant. Suddenly a flock of white birds came, covering the surface of the water for a moment; then they rose into the air forming the shape of a cross. There was a great light and the water was clear and beautiful, the boat I was in became white, Gildas was with me and I held Astra in my arms.

On April 9th, Gildas had been very near and real all day. As I sat in silence in the evening a sense of great tranquillity came to me and I knew that Gildas was kneeling beside me. He reached for my right hand and placed a ring on the third finger, then he smiled and said, 'Come to the cottage and live there in peace.' I was physically conscious of the feel of the ring which was gold and set with tiny replicas of the jewel.

The following day I attended a Quaker meeting. Before the meeting I asked Gildas to give me a subject for meditation, and he suggested 'The Light of the World'. At first it was easy to enter into the tranquillity of worship and to meditate : it came to me that light was like love, an outpouring from a source. Then Gildas said, 'Children conceived of great love have deep and lovely souls.'

At this point, someone was moved to speak, and afterwards concentration became difficult, but Gildas was beside me looking rather grave and urging me to concentrate.

I was walking in great darkness, and all around me were evil forces and figures, my only weapon against them was a flickering light which they tried continually to extinguish. I understood that only my will, if it were strong enough, could keep the light from failing. The effort of concentration became almost a physical pain, but somehow I kept on, and as long as the light burned I knew that the evil around me could do no harm. Soon I saw the luminous glow ahead, and realized it was a pool. In the middle of the pool stood Gildas, his white robe shining. I made a tremendous effort at concentration and keeping the light burning, and at last I stood on the water of the pool with Gildas. The water was beautiful and shone with a continually glowing light. Gildas spoke :

'This is the Water of Light; you must retrace your steps with a bowl of it and sprinkle the darkness with its light, but be careful that you do not spill it or use it all too soon, or you will not reach your journey's end. If your will is sufficient, the cup will not spill.'

Then Gildas gave me a silver cup filled with this glorious Water of Light, and I set out to perform my task. It was not easy, for the cup was wide and shallow, and the forces and figures about me did their utmost to make me spill it, but I sprinkled them sparingly with the water, and as I did so they disappeared. At last my journey was accomplished, and light shone all around. I looked back and saw that where I had walked and sprinkled water had now become a great lake filled with the Water of Light, and all darkness had vanished. Gildas appeared and we walked hand in hand over the surface of this Lake of Light.

Later I dreamed that I was at the cottage, making curtains. I was struck by the obvious need of cleaning and redecorating.

Marriage in the Inner World

In a village church there was a beautiful atmosphere; the organ began to play and I felt serene and at rest. Gildas was close, then he took my hand and said, 'Ruth, I need you; will you marry me on Easter Sunday?'

It seemed only right and natural to answer 'Yes', for I love Gildas dearly, but away from the atmosphere of the church I was beset by doubts and fears.

In the afternoon Gildas told me not to be afraid but to prepare quietly for the wedding with meditation and tranquillity of spirit. He also said that we must prepare the cottage that we might live there together.

At night I was conscious of Gildas lying beside me in bed, holding me gently in his arms; then he kissed me and told me that he was going to the cottage.

When I slept I dreamed that I was at the cottage with Gildas. We worked hard, scrubbing, painting, cleaning, making ready for our marriage.

On the following night, when I woke Gildas was again with me in bed, and I was once more frightened and full of doubt about these experiences. Was it madness? Hallucination? Then, as he tenderly held me and spoke of his love, I felt full of joy and love for him; all my fears vanished and I thought, 'If such joy and exaltation is madness, then my one wish for mankind is that they too may be mad and know these wonderful experiences.'

It was Easter Sunday, my twenty-second birthday and my wedding day. I had thought that our wedding would take place in our charming village church, and I attended morning service hoping to meet Gildas there. The service was beautiful and it 'spoke' to me as a Church of England service had never done before. When it was over, I felt happy and radiant and secure, yet still Gildas was not with me.

In the afternoon I felt a desperate urge to be alone, and I walked through the woods and up on to the downs, to a spot which is very special for me and to which I often go to meditate. All was peace and beauty, and I was utterly alone. I sat down on the grass—and suddenly Gildas was with me. The experience in the inner world which followed was timeless and vivid, and afterwards I knew that I was the wife of Gildas.

Gildas took my hand, and we walked in love and serenity through a long avenue of trees, silently and almost in an attitude of prayer. At the end of the avenue was a massive studded wooden door, and Gildas knocked on this three times. The door opened at his knock, and we passed into a great hall with a tiled floor. At intervals down the hall were four hexagonal shapes worked in tiles, and beside each shape stood a white-robed figure holding a bowl.

Gildas led me on to the first hexagon, and we stood inside it, facing each other. The figure holding the bowl offered it to Gildas, who took something from it and sprinkled it over me— it was earth. Then the bowl was offered to me and I sprinkled Gildas with earth in the same way. After this the robed figure went round the hexagon sprinkling earth until the bowl was empty.

We then moved to the next hexagon, where the ceremony was repeated, this time with water. At the third hexagon the bowl held fire, and at the fourth it appeared to hold nothing, but when Gildas solemnly sprinkled me with this invisible thing, I realized that it was wind. At each hexagon the ceremony was the same.

When we had left the hexagon of wind, we came to another door. Again Gildas knocked three times, and again the door opened. This time we were in the cave where I had found the jewel—with its beauty of form and vaulting—all made up of hexagons. Each section of the hexagon was bathed as before in different coloured light: red, green, blue, yellow, white, and purple, and in each section stood a choir, so that sweet music filled the air. The one difference was the fountain in the middle of the cave; this was now the fountain which had been covered in ice—the symbol of male and female combined. Gildas and I stood on opposite sides of the fountain, and this time it was Gildas, not I, who plunged his hand into it, and brought forth, not a jewel, but a simple golden wedding ring. This he put gently on the third finger of my right hand, together with the ring he had given me a few days earlier, and then hand in hand, with the beauty of the music still in our ears, we walked from the cavern—man and wife—returning to our cottage.

Gildas had said that our love could be consummated other than physically, and, after a very 'outer-worldly' day on Easter Monday at Goodwood motor races, I had a beautiful experience in the evening, alone in my room.

From time to time I have had an experience when it seemed that Gildas has come to me and taken a part of me to golden mountains in the distance, and this one on Easter Monday was similar in many respects except that more than a part of me was involved.

Gildas came to me and took my hands in his. Suddenly I felt very light, as though I had no body and had left the earth. I flew, higher and higher with Gildas, towards a golden light. Suddenly we were bathed in the light, and we ceased to 'be' as two separate people; we were one, bound in light and joy and love. Then, as suddenly, the experience was over. I was in my room sitting on the bed, and Gildas was sitting beside me holding my hands, but I felt relaxed and full of peace and well-being, and knew that I had experienced something very beautiful and real. I have had this experience several times since.

CHAPTER 7

The Second Journey

May to August 1960

On May 22nd, I was walking with Gildas on a beautiful lake of clear, sparkling water, yet somehow all was not well, and when I noticed that Gildas was wearing a black robe, I was filled with fear. Gildas turned towards me and took both my hands in his; he gazed at me intently without speaking, and into my mind came words from the twenty-third Psalm : 'Yea, though I walk through the vale of death's dark shadow, yet will I fear no evil, for Thou art with me.' Then my husband held me closely in his arms, and there was a moment of ecstasy before I felt myself sinking, alone, into the depths of the water.

Now the water was no longer clear, but cloudy and full of clinging weed. Then it changed again and I was in a deep, watery, prehistoric forest surrounded by monsters. There was choking thick growth, mud, water and monsters everywhere. I reached the mud and was beginning to sink, terrified, right into it, when something struck my hand—it was the jewel on its chain round my waist. I held it tightly, and all fear left me. I knew with great assurance that no monster would touch me, that the growth in the forest would not choke me, and that the mud would not claim me as a victim. As the feeling flowed through me I relaxed, and instead of sinking into the mud, I found a stepping stone and stood firmly upon it. I noticed other stepping stones forming a kind of path through the thick forest. Suddenly I knew what task it was that lay ahead of me : with the aid of the jewel and the stepping stones I must fight my way through to clear water once more. Holding tightly to the jewel I set out on my journey.

For many days the struggle through the forest continued. As well as being an exhausting experience, it was a very 'real' one for it was there both in full consciousness (I had only to close my eyes) and at night in dreams.

Then it changed: the monsters were gone, and instead of the thick growth which threatened to strangle me, there were wicked thorns which tore my flesh at every step. The mud was thick and sticky, and it became so dark that I could not see. I could only struggle blindly on, and always there was with me a fear—the fear of finding something dead. The forest was cold, too, and I felt alone, cut off from all things.

All the time I prayed desperately for light and protection. The fear and panic were worst when I was in bed at night. Dr. Swainson had suggested that I should make the symbol of the cross in a circle, above me, in light, to aid me in the hours of darkness. I tried many times to do this, but I was unable to make the circle of light complete; there was always at least one patch of darkness where the light would not shine.

One night in mid-June I was trying once again to make the circle of light around the cross—when suddenly it was complete, glowing strongly, but it was not I who had made it. It was as if Dr. Swainson were with me, in my room, radiating light to help me. The black struggle in the forest went on, but at least there was a contact, I was not so alone. Some of my despair lifted. Now I seemed to move quite steadily, pace by pace instead of inch by inch, but the experience was still agony, and my body torn, scratched and bleeding. All day the inner experiences seemed to invade the outer world and I had waves of sickness. Yet through it all was the feeling of something sustaining me— enabling me to cope with daily living. The coldness had almost gone and, though weak, I was determined to come through.

The Rock and the Creatures

Now I came to another obstacle in the darkness—something in the way—it *felt* like a rock. Desperately I trampled round in the mud, the thorns still tearing me at every step, trying to find a way past the obstacle. I asked for light in order to be able to see clearly what the obstacle might be. A flash of light was granted, and in it I saw a huge rock and high up in it a hole or cave. I knew that I must climb up the almost sheer rock face to the cave. Three times I attempted the gruelling ascent, and three times I failed. Then at last at the fourth attempt I reached the cave, which had a ledge outside. To my horror I found the cave was full of slimy, flat, fishy-snaky creatures, and I knew I could not go on until they were out of the way. I asked for help, and found that I was holding a net into which the revolting creatures must be gathered. This was worse than the mud; the things were repulsive in the extreme; they stuck to me and covered me as I endeavoured to put them into the net. They tried, too, to escape over the ledge, but I knew that if they got lost in this way I should have to go and find them.

I prayed for light, and it came in the form of a thunderstorm with great flashes of lightning. When the lightning flashed I could see to get the creatures into the net—though so ugly were the reptiles that I would almost rather have continued in darkness. My task seemed never-ending; the cave seemed packed with the vile mass. Suddenly it began to rain; I was glad, for the creatures now became more slimy and slippery and didn't stick to me as much. Then, to my horror, with the aid of a terrific flash of lightning, I saw three of them sliding over the ledge. I tried to stop them, but over they went into the mud below. I knew I should have to go down and fetch them, so with great hesitation and trembling I jumped off the ledge—back into the mud and thorns below. Wearily I groped around trying to find the creatures; it seemed an impossible task in such thick mud and darkness, with only the lightning to help. I was filled with hopelessness; why did my desperate prayers for light remain unanswered? Supposing I were to fail the test? To fail my dearest love, Gildas? To fail to come forth into the light again? I was frightened and alone, yet still I found the strength to cling to the jewel, to pray, and to remember that I was being surrounded with thoughts of love and light even though I was unable to contact them.

All the time I was going back over the path I had already

trodden. I prayed again for light and at last it came, as a gentle ray. The thunder and lightning stopped, and in this new and gentler light I could see a tree, and beneath the tree the three creatures which I sought. I approached slowly through the mud, and then saw that the place was guarded by a dragon—hairy, fierce and horrid to behold. I asked for weapons, for I knew the dragon must be overcome, but my request was not granted. Instead I knew that if only I could remember the Lord's Prayer the battle would be over. I tried to say it, but my mind seemed dull and lethargic, and my memory failed me. The dragon was darkness itself—and somehow the light must prove the stronger. I concentrated hard upon the gentle ray of light, then suddenly there were voices about me, saying the Lord's Prayer, reminding me of the familiar phrases. Slowly and haltingly I recited the lovely words, and as I did so the dragon vanished—overcome. I put the three reptiles into my net and set out again for the rock.

The light had now gone, but I was stronger, less weary. I noticed that I walked easily, on firm ground instead of mud, and the thorns were no longer about me. I soon reached the rock and prepared for the hard ascent, but, groping in the darkness, I found a rope and ascended to the cave with comparative ease, always bearing the net. With renewed vigour I set to work to collect the creatures, almost forgetting their repulsiveness. Quite soon the task was complete, the net full, and I entered the cave, going forward at last. Soon it became impossible to stand, and the passage became so narrow that the only way to progress was to pull myself forward on my stomach, dragging the net behind. Progress was slow and difficult—painful too—for the passage was rough and I was continually grazed as I moved forward, on and on into the darkness. This continued, ever in the background of my daily life, for five nights and five days, but in the evening of the fifth day, as I sat quietly in meditation, there was a great rumbling and quaking, and the rock through which I was passing was seized with earthquake tremors. Great cracks appeared, and I had to go forward as quickly as possible, desperately hoping that the piece of rock to which I clung would not split. Enormous crevices appeared every second beneath my body, yet still the confined tunnel was there and I must follow it as best I could, taking care not to lose my precious net.

It was now mid-July. The following notes are taken from a daily diary which I wrote for Dr. Swainson.

... Still crawling through cracking rock. It is a most perilous journey and takes a good deal of energy, but I am strong and determined.

... Now the fear of finding something dead has returned. I feel at times as if I would gladly go on through cracking rock for ever, but soon, I know, all will change, and I'm terrified of what may be ahead.

... Horrible experience last night. I woke up, about 2 a.m., to hear all kinds of strange noises in the air around me and somehow *inside* my head. It was extremely dark and I was panic-stricken; I wanted to scream, but seemed unable to do so. I began to shake and tremble with fright. Suddenly, through the noises about me, I heard a different sound, a gentle yet commanding voice which said, 'Ruth, sit up, put on the light, and be calm and still.' I tried to sit up, but could not; then came the voice again, and with it strength from within. With a great effort I sat up straight and put on the light. Then I remembered your advice about meditation; I sat as straight as could be—polarized to God—and willed myself to be 'calm and still'. Gradually the noises about and within me receded and ceased, and all was peace. After about half an hour I was ready to sleep, but first felt the need to seal the seven centres. This I did, and soon slept—really deep, restful sleep, undisturbed even by dreams of the 'valley of the shadow'.

... Little change, though the cracking of the rock seems more violent with every inch I travel, so my terror increases. I feel like having a jolly good 'let off steam' at someone—and I know *you* won't *mind*! (Did so on paper.)

... Still feeling somewhat vicious ... I don't feel strong any longer—just miserable and weak and frightened.

... The journey is changing! I'm so frightened, and still I can't see very much, but the cracking and trembling have stopped, and I don't seem to be going through rock any more. I'm still wiggling through a narrow tunnel, but it seems to be through earth rather than rock. I feel stronger than I did yesterday.

... On and on through the now earthy tunnel. At times the earth is so soft that it caves in and makes a blockage, so that I have to dig through it with my hands. The tunnel seems to be going downwards, though very gradually. If only there were a glimmer of light ahead, but all is darkness. I still have my net of creatures with me.

The Fall to the Cave

For over a week there was no change. Then suddenly there seemed to be nothing ahead, and I began to fall quickly down a kind of 'chimney'. I was terrified that I would hurt myself on landing, for I was falling very fast. I struggled and flung out arms and legs in an attempt to gain some kind of steadying hold, but all to no avail, and twice I almost lost my net of creatures. After a day or so, I found I could relax and then, instead of falling quickly, I began to float gently down this shaft. The awful panic left me, and at last I found a breathing space in which to gain strength for whatever was to come. But still all was dark, and I longed for light.

The following day I came gently to rest at the bottom of the shaft, but to my horror I found I was paralysed—unable to move at all. I lay in the darkness, terrified again and helpless; all I could do was to pray and remember that the Light *would* triumph in the end, but how long I could remain calm and courageous when the way seemed unending I did not know. I was not holding the jewel, for I could not move my hands towards it. I tried to picture it above and before me, but this required a great effort of will and sapped my strength greatly.

For nine days I remained completely paralysed, until on the ninth I had an accident in the outer world, falling off a scooter, and was in hospital with an injury to my eye. At least this gave an opportunity to give time and energy to the journey, and was a turning point.

On the day following the accident, suddenly I found that I could move. No longer was I terrified, but felt loved and protected. I grasped the jewel with both hands and would have got up and tried to proceed on my journey, but a voice in the darkness spoke: 'Rest, my child, for you are very weary. Peace will surround you; there is nothing to fear. You have yet other things to endure, but first be filled with strength. Sleep peacefully and well.' At these words I began to relax and soon I was sleeping—renewing strength.

I continued resting peacefully until ten days later, when I felt a tremendous urge to go up to my 'special place'. Though still rather weary after the accident, I made the effort to go. In the quiet of this beautiful place I was surrounded with strength, and for a while all was as before in the inner world: I watched while a part of me slept. Then, suddenly, I was wholly in the inner world, awakening from my long and strength-giving rest. It was still very dark, but in my hand was a sword, and gradually I was aware of something glowing in the darkness. All around me were great luminous eyes and teeth, presumably belonging to some evil creatures—but the other parts of their bodies were lost in the utter blackness around me. I struck out with the sword at the point where I judged the creatures' necks might be; I was unsuccessful at every stroke and had an eerie feeling that these heads were not attached to bodies—they seemed to float around me. I was still very strong after my rest, and I noticed that as I struck out there was an air of panic in the cave, as though these things knew that eventually they would die by my sword. At last a stroke went home, the glow left two eyes and one set of teeth, and a lifeless head fell with a dull thud to the ground. At this moment the cave which formed the bottom of the shaft became filled with a warm soft light. Looking for the source of light, I found that it came from the net which had once contained the slimy creatures which I had hated so much; a most lovely transformation had taken place, and the ugliness within the net was no more. Instead there was a beautiful glowing sphere, and the things which I had once thought so black had become a source of light. I released the sphere from the net, and it floated above and to the left of me, so that now I could see and my task was therefore made easier. The creatures' heads were not really unattached to their bodies, but they had long necks, and it was the movement of these which in the darkness had made the heads seem to float about me. They were strange figures, covered in hair, with long flat bodies and short pointed legs almost like inadequate flippers. They were foolish creatures and, now I could see, were not difficult to kill. Nevertheless I was glad to leave the cave behind me.

The Pool of Blood and the Bones

I emerged into a world which was rather hazy. I was aware of a pool of blood, some black and white bulls, and a horrible, wizened man-like creature. But still the beautiful sphere of light was with me.

It was now mid-August, and I spent a week-end at Dr. Swainson's house to do some intensive work on the journey.

In meditation, on the Friday evening, I saw all this more clearly. There was a pool of blood, and in the middle an island. On the right hand side of the pool in a bare brown enclosure lived some black and white bulls. On the left of the pool there was luxuriant grass. The bulls, driven by hunger, endeavoured to go to the luscious grass, but on the island in the middle of the pool dwelt an evil and wizened man who shot them with poisoned darts as they went. As they lay dying, great birds swooped from above and tore the carcasses until the blood drained from them and joined that already in the pool.

I was horrified. Blood has always held terror for me, and I felt that I must wade through this pool to the island and kill the miserable creature who dwelt there, thus freeing the bulls. I stood quaking and terrified on the edge, trying to find the strength and courage to accomplish this repulsive task. Then again, in the midst of my fear and hesitation, came a voice: 'Do not hurry, my child; and do not be ashamed of your fear.'

On the Saturday morning, soon after I woke, Gildas was with me. He stayed only a few moments—but those moments gave me great strength. 'It will not be much longer now, my dear one. I am watching and waiting.' He kissed me and was gone.

Again in meditation I saw the scene with the pool of blood, the bulls and the horrid little man. From somewhere I found the strength and will to wade through the pool of blood to the island; but, once there, the realization came to me: this is no creature to be killed by the sword, but a man to be transformed with light and love. Then I knew that the whole scene in all its ugliness could be transformed into one of beauty.

The pool would become water, clear and lovely; the ugly man a water spirit, guardian of the pool and a part of its beauty. There would be luscious greenness everywhere and the black and white bulls would be free to wander where they pleased. The birds of prey would become birds of peace; there would be harmony instead of disharmony.

I knew that it would need great strength and light and love to make this vision reality. I called upon all the powers of light to come to my aid. My prayer was most marvellously answered: there was love and light everywhere, and after a period of deep concentration and 'giving out', I knew that the wonderful transformation had taken place. I was free to go on my way, leaving behind a place of beauty, strength and peace.

Further along the path I came to a desert, and a little child put his hand trustingly in mine. 'Please take me across the desert.' But the desert was bleak and lonely and a great storm was coming up.

In the evening, although I had passed the pool of blood in the inner world, it felt heavy and unresolved within me, and I knew that I must work on it with Dr. Swainson. As we talked, a persistent image came before me, of a narrow street, with tall houses and deep gutters running with blood. Everywhere women were rushing about screaming, and men were trying to comfort them. The women were dressed in crinoline-type dresses and the men wore tight trousers and jackets with tight sleeves. I was filled with terror and nausea, yet still I did not know why there was blood in the streets nor what was being killed.

Then, quite suddenly, without the image changing, I knew. Children were being killed—massacred by soldiers, and it was their blood which ran in the streets.

Slowly the image left me—likewise the terror and nausea— and soon I felt quite light and 'floaty', as if a great weight had been lifted from me.

During the night I dreamed that I was crossing the desert with the child, a little boy of about four years old. A great storm blew up, and there was sand and wind everywhere. The child was terribly frightened, and so was I. Then I gradually realized that in order to calm the child's fear I myself must be unafraid. Slowly my fear left me as I sought to comfort the child and make him secure. On we went; sometimes I would carry the child, sometimes he would walk. Soon the wind and the storm died down and the desert became very hot, but on we went for what seemed a very long time, until we reached a garden, a beautiful place of peace. Here, the child told me, he wished to remain, and the place seemed so lovely I wished that I too might remain there, but I could not, I must go on; so I went, leaving a happy child behind me.

Beyond the desert was a great fire through which I had to pass—but this I knew from before, and I had little fear as I walked calmly and unharmed through the roaring flames.

Beyond the fire was a river, black and unpleasant, winding away into the distance. At the bank of the river was a boat. I was faced with a choice : I could go down the river by boat, or I could swim. I was afraid and unsure as to which choice would be right.

The following morning (Sunday) I felt frightened and uneasy, yet did not know what it was I feared.

In meditation I saw again the river and the boat, and faced the choice once more. I decided to swim—and how glad I was afterwards that I had made this choice! I pushed the boat out from the bank; it floated on its own a little way down the river, then great waves troubled the water, the boat was caught in some weed, soon the waves filled it and it sank to the depths of the river.

The sword was still with me, so I took it and began to swim down the river, though it was certainly more difficult to swim with the sword. Everywhere there were weeds which I must cut through with the sword before I could move forward. Soon I realized that the river went through three 'phases'. First it was cold, almost freezing, so that I could hardly move; then it became unbearably hot; and lastly it would become rough and turbulent with great waves.

I came to a place where branches of trees were interlaced on the surface of the water so that I had to swim beneath them. The river went through its cold phase, and I felt still, frozen, hardly able to move.

Before me I saw something which filled me with horror: the 'something dead' which I had dreaded throughout the journey. There were bruised, crushed, human bodies floating on the water, and on each side of the river were rocks, covered with bones. Between the rocks was a narrow passageway of water through which I must pass. Now I realized that the bodies belonged to those who had been caught in this passageway at the turbulent phase of the river, when they had been battered and crushed upon the rocks by the rushing waters. Deliberately I found something to cling to and waited until the crashing waves had passed; then, as the river chilled, I began to make my way through the narrow, rock-bound gulley. It was a difficult battle —my body almost froze at every stroke, but I was determined to progress and reach the end before the river's next rough phase. Now the water became hot; I knew that little time was left— and now a thick barrier of weeds barred my way. I slashed out desperately with my sword in the scalding hot water, and bit by bit I advanced. At last the end of the rocks was in sight, and with the roar of the oncoming waves in my ears, I swam clear of the gulley and found a hold among the weeds as the waves crashed and foamed around me.

On the Sunday afternoon, in meditation, I was in the water once more, still clinging to a reed. Now I knew I must go forward again—and I had a strong feeling that the time of blackness was almost at an end. After a talk with Dr. Swainson about the 'bones', the river no longer had its three phases, though it was still black and there were still many weeds through which to cut my way. In a little while I came to a great face of rock, and wondered how to get past it. Then I realized that the water went right underneath it. I dived down, down, into the depths and the blackness, until at last I could swim underneath the rock. It was very thick, and it took some time to come through to the other side, yet when I did, the water was no longer black but clear. There were still many weeds about me and above me, but I felt the need to rise to the surface, and I began to work my way upwards, cutting the weeds as I went. As I swam on up and up, I felt an impulse to drop the sword, even though still surrounded with weeds. I did so, and suddenly it needed no effort to rise; I just floated upwards, and as I went the weeds about me parted and sprang into flower. The water was clear, silvery and full of light; my body felt washed, rested and renewed, and all scars of the journey disappeared. Lighter and lighter I became until, reaching the surface of the water, I continued to float upward through the air, clothed in flowing gold and bathed in light. My arms were stretched out and upward, in a cup-like shape; then looking up I saw Gildas descending towards me, also clothed in gold and bathed in light, but he was straight and upright as he came. Then I knew that we were—had become—that symbol of male and female united, the golden fountain. I was the feminine, the chalice; Gildas the masculine, the phallic symbol, the point of the fountain; and about us light flowed everywhere. Gildas took my hand and together we floated on and on until we came at last to a place of peace, green and beautiful, and there we remained.

CHAPTER 8

Interlude Between Journeys

August 1960 to February 1961

The second journey ended on August 21st. In the morning of the
22nd Gildas brought Astra to me, and I was astonished to find
that she had grown; she was no longer a baby but a beautiful
child of about five years old.

At home again, later in the day, in the quiet of the garden,
Gildas came and spoke gently to me :

'You have laboured for a long and weary time, my love, and
now you must rest completely in the peace of this lovely place.
When you are ready we will go together to the cottage, for you
have yet much to learn about the children there, but all that is
for the future; you must do nothing until you are well and
strong again. I know that you are feeling radiant and full of
light, but during the time of blackness you have given much out
and have grown weary in the struggle, with a weariness that does
not pass easily or quickly.

'Also, Ruth, remember that I love you dearly, that *I* have
missed *you*, and this time of peace together will be a great joy
to me—to us both I hope. It will be a time when our love will
grow and strengthen and will find new depths of tenderness, new
joys of expression.

'One thing you may do here, and that is to get to know Astra.
I' have talked of you often to her, and she longs to know and to
love her mother. Our child is beautiful, Ruth, happy and good,
but you must be gentle with her and realize that she hardly
knows you; and you must try, too, not to feel unhappy if at first
she should turn more readily to me than to you, for soon, with

patient love and care, she will know you well and together you will find great joy in that special love which exists between mother and daughter.

'I want you to be quite quiet here, and patient, and just "be". I know you have many questions to ask, but most of them will wait until the time when you are ready to absorb my teaching in serenity and confidence, free from the background of strain, after a period of true rest.'

'Gildas, please may I ask one question? Need that time of weariness and darkness have been so long?'

'My dear, questions about time are very difficult for us to answer, for our time is not as yours, and we find it hard to judge. You can tell from the change in Astra that your struggle has lasted a far longer time in the inner world than in the outer, and you have often been aware during this time that a particular task or battle has seemed to cover months in the inner world—yet in the outer only a comparatively short time has passed.

'If you could have found the strength—and sufficient time in which to be quiet—then you could have worked through this much more quickly as regards outer time, though the time in the inner world would have remained the same. Yet to work through in a shorter time requires as much, and perhaps more, strength than when it is drawn out as your struggle was. It is true that the effort is more concentrated and therefore all is more quickly over, but if you had worked in this way you would have needed a long period in which to "come to the surface" once more, and in this way the time of strain would hardly have been shorter, and you would have been unable to come immediately to this place of peace. A soul must come gradually back from the depths, lest it leave any of its strength behind, or bring with it any of the darkness it has known. I know that you came back relatively quickly, but then you took the journey slowly, and, though you may not have felt it, you were coming at every step nearer to the Light.

'You could, then, have made one deeply concentrated effort and have passed the uttermost blackness quite quickly, but with great output of strength, and there would have been need of a long transition period before you came fully into the Light.

'Rest now, my dearest love, and I will remain here beside you, helping you to take into yourself the stillness of this place.'

Astra and the Teddy Bear

On August 23rd I talked for a while with Astra, telling her that I had been to a dark place where I had had to work, but that I had often thought of her with great love, and was now glad to be back with her and Gildas again, and that I hoped the three of us would have some lovely times together. I told her, too, that I had been helped in my work by another person in the outer world whom she might know as her 'grandmother', and that her grandmother would like to send her a present.

Astra thought for a while, then said, 'Please tell her that I'd like a great huge Teddy Bear.' I let Dr. Swainson know what she had asked for.

On the night of the 24th I was not very sleepy. About 11 p.m. Astra came to me to show me her new Teddy Bear, and, when I had admired it, I wrote down, there and then, in a notebook:

'Astra showed me her Teddy Bear. He is white, with a lovely face and furry ears, a blue bow round his neck, and he growls a lovely deep growl when turned on his tummy. She wants to know what he is called. He is almost as big as herself—well not quite—but she's very thrilled.'

On the 25th, the morning *after* I had seen the Teddy Bear in the inner world, I received a letter from Dr. Swainson in which she described the 'thought image' she had made of the bear: 'He is called "Polar Bear" and he is quite white and about two feet high when his legs are stretched out, but of course they bend so that he sits down, and he has a very nice expression and nice furry ears.' (So all was correct, except for the blue bow and the deep growl which she had not thought of!)

Later, Gildas brought Astra to me and we had a happy time playing together with the Teddy Bear. She said she was pleased with his name 'Polar Bear', and asked me to send 'that grand-mummy about 150 kisses!'

Making a Light Centre

On August 24th I had felt full of light and knew that I could radiate it into the world. I spent quite a long time doing this, praying that rays might go wherever there was darkness. Later on, as I sat quietly meditating, I had a vision in which I saw utter blackness, seemingly impenetrable. Then at last I knew that at its centre was a strong glowing light. Slowly the light overcame the darkness and became very bright and exceedingly beautiful. But then I saw in its centre a sphere of blackness, yet the blackness had no power to mar the beauty of the light. Words came to me, 'In darkness is light, in light, darkness.'

That night (after Astra had shown me her Teddy Bear at 11 p.m.) I slept for a while, but at 2 a.m. I woke. There was a feeling of evil and coldness in the room, and I was afraid. Soot fell down the chimney and an icy wind blew through the window; somewhere in the house a door slammed. Suddenly I saw that I was ringed with a circle of light and in the circle was a cross. Then Gildas was beside me, giving out light calmly and strongly. Gently he told me to sit up straight and to concentrate on raising myself towards the Light. Soon the feeling of evil left the room, and I felt warmth and peace about me instead. I lay down, and Gildas stayed beside me until I slept again.

The following day I asked Gildas about the experience.

'Yesterday there was a great deal of light here in this house and about you, and the more you sent it out, the more strongly it glowed all round here. Now, wherever there is a strong light, especially in a place which has not before been hallowed or sacred, the forces of darkness are also attracted, and attempt to battle, as it were, for possession. There is no need to fear, if you surround yourself with light and consciously "lift" yourself, for the light is stronger than the darkness, and will always triumph.'

* * * * *

On September 22nd 1960, Gildas told me that Astra was to have a brother. He was conceived on September 4th.

* * * * *

The Schism between the Two Worlds

Despite the happiness in the inner world, by the end of November the two worlds were beginning to draw dangerously apart. One day I found that, almost unconsciously, I had written the two following passages, the first in much fainter script than the second, and both in somewhat large, scrawling script :

'I, the spirit, am weary for heavenly lands and pastures of joy. The world is wearisome to me, and I cry and pray continually for the end of this dreary exile. O to live always with thee, my dear one, in the world which I see now but fleetingly. O gentle death, come soon—O soon.'

'I am the earth with magnetic pull—the body. I want to live. Earthly bodily pleasures are sweet to me. I want marriage and earthly children. I want real and tangible experience, and to that end I will shun the "airy fairy". I will rejoice in all that is "animal"; I will seek the sensations and thrills of living and will hold to life with all my strength.'

At the time I was having three dreams which were repeated every night :

(1) I dreamed that I was being pulled in half by two forces. Afterwards the two parts of me could not find each other, and when they eventually did, they would no longer fit.

(2) There was a mountain with a road up each side of it, leading to a beautiful house or church. The road on the right was steep and icy and therefore impassable. The road on the left was too steep to climb and there was no middle way.

(3) As the second dream, but this time the roads on the right and left had a sign 'No Through Road', and there was a middle way which ascended in a spiral to the beautiful place. It was obviously the road to take but as soon as I stepped on to it, it was lost.

In a therapy session with Dr. Swainson we worked on the dreams and on this division between the two worlds. In meditation with her, I went into the dream of the three roads, and was once more lost after stepping on to the middle road. Suddenly there was a great light, and a voice which said, 'Travellers must travel upon the road and not wander from the pathway.' I replied that I had lost the road, and was told to go back and find my Guide.

I returned and found Gildas waiting for me. 'My dear,' he said, 'the time for travelling alone is over, and you must learn now to accept help in finding the road. Remember I cannot come to you; you must come and ask for my aid.'

CHAPTER 9

The Third Journey and the Dedication

February to September 1961

Towards the end of February I was sitting quietly at home, when I had an urgent wish to talk to Gildas, although for two or three weeks I had been avoiding him. Almost immediately he was with me in the inner world.

'Oh Ruth, at last you are receptive and ready to talk to me. I have watched you lately with much anxiety, my dear; you are so troubled and unhappy and generally "out of tune". You seem to need me and yet you avoid me; confide in me if you can, and face up to whatever is troubling you. You know I love you and know you, and always will, and I hate to see you as you are now.'

'Gildas, I don't know what is the matter with me; I feel awful. I ache inside and feel tense and stretched as if I shall break, and with it all there is a great weariness and a dread of some dark thing close at hand.'

'The dread of the dark thing I can explain to you. I told you that you had chosen a difficult way. When a soul comes into the world again, it is able to choose to some extent the way it will tread. You have lived before, my dear, and we have known each other in other lives. I knew and loved you briefly on earth, and afterwards as your Guide. One day you may remember these things, but in this life you have much to suffer and learn. The six-sided symbol has great power for you, but it is also a symbol of six "journeys" in darkness and trial which you must take.

128

Each will seem darker and harder to bear than the last—but when you win through (and you *will* come through)—you will know the Truth and the reason for it all. You have gained two sides of the hexagon, but soon you must try the third. Our son whom you carry will be born in great pain and tribulation and there is much darkness to follow. But this time I need not leave you and we shall win through together. You are strong, and all the powers of Light will come to your aid should you need them.

'This is the "dark thing" which you feel close at hand; but the "ache" is something which you must recognize and face up to yourself. It is hard I know, and I know how miserable you feel. It hurts to face things, dearest, but when you do healing can take place and things can be put right.

'Just another thing: you need far more quietness, Ruth, and time to be true to yourself. If you are going to lead a gay superficial life, you must also have time for more serious things and for the inner things too; you must try to bring together and to recognize all the time the value of each. Each in its own place, but not entirely separated from the other.

'I have told you some hard things, my loved one, and you are tired. Don't avoid me, come and rest in my love.'

Preparation for the Journey

Four days later, Gildas was with me again.

'Ruth, I know how difficult it is to give more time to quietness and meditation, but I am very serious when I say that at present you *need* more time. The journey which you are about to undertake will require great strength; you will be tried to the very end of your endurance; there will be times when it seems impossible ever to return to a world of light. I am not trying to frighten you unnecessarily, dear, but I know the peril that lies ahead. You must never seriously doubt that you will come through, but you must also be prepared for a hard road full of suffering and loneliness. You will have companions in love and sympathy, for I will be with you in the inner world and Mary will be with you in the outer, but *still* you will feel desperately alone in the darkness.

'The time for this journey is very near, and your preparation must be in meditation and quietness of spirit. Forget for a time your fear, and learn faith and trust. In times that you set aside for quietness I will come to you, and in preparation for the darkness we will journey briefly in search of Light. Thus you will become calm, strong and serene, ready for the path you have to tread.'

Later, Gildas spoke to me about diet.

'Ruth, during the coming darkness the kind of food which you eat can play quite an important part. Eating the wrong food can in itself produce feelings of darkness in the inner world.

'You need fresh vegetables and fruit, eggs, cheese and milk. Eat only brown bread—and not too much of it, and have brown sugar instead of white. Honey is a good food and nuts are sustaining, but do not eat too much meat. Fruit juice is better than tea to drink and has in it some of the warmth and light of the sun which ripened the fruit. Eat all these things and you will be strengthened for your journey.'

For five days I walked with Gildas in a warm and sunny place, high in the mountains, filled with light and tranquillity. We bathed in gentle streams and walked with tireless feet on smooth paths. We breathed air which was scented with the perfume of many flowers and filled with lovely music. When we slept we knew no fear and awoke strong and refreshed. All was harmony and peace; for a while the dark shadow slipped from me and I knew that in some wonderful way I was being prepared and strengthened for the path ahead.

Finally Gildas led me to a green valley, and there we sat quiet and still. Soon I felt, rather than saw, the presence of many beings radiating light, and I heard again the voice:

'Go, my child. You have chosen the way you would tread; it is a dark and perilous path—yet you are strong and have a worthy Guide. Remember, too, that all our aid is at hand should you need it to win in the darkest hour. Hold the jewel and all will be well.'

As the voice faded I felt a circle of coloured light surrounding Gildas and me; then slowly we began to float away from the beautiful land.

Gildas took my hands and clasped them over the jewel hanging on its chain at my waist. 'Don't be afraid; we shall return when the journey is over.'

The Journey Begins

Now we started to fall, and it grew cold. We were falling slowly but it was an unpleasant sensation. Soon we reached the ground and began to go forward through a thick mist. It was March 3rd when the journey began, and a fortnight later we were still walking through the mist which became thicker and thicker. There was an acrid smell and the mist turned to clouds of stifling yellow smoke. Now the ground was rocky and the going hard. Soon I noticed huge cracks which grew gradually wider and then flames poured forth from the depths of the earth. Then we went more slowly, for these gaps had to be crossed. I was afraid of being burned and felt heavy and without hope.

A week passed during which it had been growing steadily darker, and finally it became quite black. I could no longer see Gildas—only feel his presence and his hand on mine. In spite of the smell and the flames and the cracks getting ever wider, I felt more calm and accepting, determined to accomplish the way I had chosen, and some of the awful heaviness left me. While teaching at school, however, I found it hard to hold on to my calmness and acceptance. I felt so terribly out of contact with the outer world, and routine tasks required a great effort of mind. It became more difficult to keep a written record, and my last entry, at the end of March, described how Gildas and I were crossing a great chasm from which flames poured, but even as we crossed it, it grew wider, and I felt myself falling into the depths. The smoke grew thicker; the flames were fierce and very hot. After falling for a long while, I landed on a ledge and Gildas was beside me. He held my hand firmly. 'Courage, my dear, I am with you, but I'm afraid we must climb out again for our way does not yet lead downwards. We must go first to the mountain of fire.' Wearily I began to climb; the sides of the chasm were rough and there were many holds, but the top was a long way off.

The Turnings to the Left and the Birth of Michael Arthor

Now I could no longer write but only tell Mary when I saw her. She wrote down what I said, and here are the records. In early May:

'It was an awful long way up. We climbed up on to another ledge. I was absolutely exhausted and really in despair. Then Gildas talked to me for a while and reminded me of having set out on a journey; we were nearer to the light than we were at the beginning, and all the time we would be getting nearer no matter how black it seemed. I slept for a little while. When I woke up I started to climb again through smoke and flames. Then we reached the top again, and we just went on walking through the blackness and the smoke and the cracks. Then on the left we came to a wall of rock; it was so dark that we walked along beside it, feeling our way. I felt so weary and heavy and frightened and horrified to think that the child would be born in the darkness. There were turnings off to the left every now and again, and I wanted so much to follow them but Gildas said I mustn't. There seemed to be something drawing me towards them. After a while, we lay down to sleep again. Whilst I was asleep I had a dream—it seemed like a dream. I dreamed that I left Gildas and followed one of these turnings, and when I woke up the dream was true. There was this tremendous pull to keep going towards the left. I could hear Gildas calling, but there seemed to be no direction. Every time I try to find out the direction of his voice it seems to be different. And that's where we are now; I'm moving the way the pull is.'

Mary and I sat in meditation; afterwards I told her :

'At first it was the same as before. Then I knew that I had to stand still. So I tried, managing it for a few minutes in spite of the pull. In those few minutes I could hear Gildas' voice much more clearly. Then all kinds of things seemed to come and push and pick and pull; I don't know what they were—couldn't see them. And voices round about, some threatening, some persuading, all wanting me to go to the left. At first I couldn't resist them. Suddenly I found some strength from somewhere; I grasped hold of the jewel and absolutely *demanded* light. It came. I was standing in a circle of light absolutely still. Things —black-looking things—were there, beyond the circle of light. I remained still and Gildas came and found me. Then we started back the other way, to the main path again. Gildas says we have to go down, and we have to go to the left, but not yet. We have to go to the mountain first.'

I saw Mary again on May 13th and told her :

'I got back on to the right path. The light stayed with us for a little while and then it began to fade slowly. We kept walking along, and then it just got blacker and blacker until it was this awful blackness, "blacker than black", impossible to describe. And I can't see anything, nor feel Gildas. I can't even move. And the child is being born.'

By May 16th I was able to say :

'Before the baby was born, the heaviness and the darkness were about me all the time, no matter what I did. They kept coming over me in terrific waves. After the birth, it's *there*, in the inner world, but I can be free of it if I want to.'

In meditation with Mary :

'I went down into the blackness. It was just as black for a while, then, quite slowly and gradually it all began to lift and it went on lifting until, although dark, it was nothing in comparison to what it was before. I don't feel paralysed any longer. I feel so light and free and so centred, too; I'm absolutely at one with myself. And I am able to be with Gildas again. He is very pleased with the baby—his son. And he said that now we shall have to go on again.' (In January 1962 the boy was named Michael Arthor.)

At the end of May :

'We went on. That's all that's happening, really. It's a very desolate place that we are going through. At first I was terribly worried about the baby, that he would have to go through all this with us. Gildas said it was all right because although he is there, and the baby will be there too, it is only I who experience all these things. Gildas is carrying the baby. It's a lovely little boy with black hair and blue eyes.'

Talks with Gildas

I had been feeling cut off and alone, because I no longer have a definite membership of a religious group. I was frightened, too, and, on entering the village church at home had been

seized with panic and the desire to run away. I asked Gildas
about this problem.

'Dear child, this is no time to be worrying about such things.
I do not want you to think I pass this off as trivial, but you are
employed on a long and difficult task which requires much
energy, and you would be wise to avoid other worries until this
is over. I know you seek the strength and companionship which
comes from true membership of a religious group, but do have
faith, my dear, and know that you are most wonderfully loved
and guided. You in the earth world fret and worry over things
which are already planned and taken care of. A little more
patience and faith in the ability of "those on the other side" to
know what is right, and when, would not come amiss. The
answer will come, Ruth; remember that all things work together
for good, at the last.

'You have a new conception of the inner journey and with it
has come a lessening of pain; yet do not let it bring also a lessening of the desire to go forward; you must work just as hard and
give just as much time to the task as before. I know it is difficult,
I know it is dreary, but look beyond, my love, to the joy and
blessed peace to come.'

'I am sorry, Gildas, you are right, of course, I have given less
time lately to quietness and the "inner things", but with your
help I will once more give all I can towards the accomplishment
of this journey. One thing, though, which I ought to have asked
before : how best can Mary help ?

'I have told you before that Mary is a "companion in love
and sympathy", and one of the best ways in which she helps is in
her understanding, and her readiness to discuss these things and
to help you to accept them with a quiet mind. Mary gives you
confidence in those areas where I cannot do so, and without her
you would be lonely indeed. Tell Mary everything, Ruth, for
then you will be reassured and helped to a serene approach to
your task.

'The meditation which you have together is good; two are
always stronger than one. The "tuning in" is good, too, as it
makes at least one point in the day when you *know* there is a
focus of light and that you are not wholly alone. Mary is helping

you faithfully and well and will always be there; give her my love and thanks, and may the Light surround and protect you both, always.'

Later, I asked Gildas about this thing of which I am frightened, and which feels like a 'knot' in my stomach, making me feel sick and shivery.

'My dear child, it grieves me to see you suffering so, but I am afraid I can give little help here. These things are painful to work through, but if I were to tell you what it is, it would not be so effective as if you go right through this and discover it yourself, hard though it may be. Mary's help is of the greatest value here; she will guide you as gently as possible to the necessary depth from which this must be uprooted. Do not work too much on it alone; you may feel deep distress and shock when all is finally unearthed, and it is desirable that you should be with someone who will understand and accept.'

The Mountain of Fire

It was now the end of June; I had dreams all night, the colour nightmare three times, and—in between—inner-world experiences of hurrying towards the mountain of fire. We ran; it was hard work, and I stumbled frequently. Gildas gave me his hand and held the baby in the other. We seemed to go on for ages—days and weeks (though in outer-world time it could only have been quite a short interval)—always hurrying, never resting, until at last we came to the foot of the fire mountain. Here Gildas spoke:

'For a while you may rest, my child, but then you must climb these black slopes. At the top you will be faced with an agonizing ordeal—and one which you must endure alone. It will not be long, but it is perhaps the most painful upon the way. I and the baby will come to the top of the mountain with you. Do not be afraid—you have great strength and all the help you need; we will hold you in love and light (though you may not be conscious of it), and we will never let you fall by the way. We know your strength, and you will not be tried beyond that. Trust me, my love, and go forward in serenity.'

The rest did not last long. By July 3rd we were climbing. The mountain was black and there was no life there at all.

While I was doing some 'free writing' for Mary, on a psychological level, the following completely different passage 'came through':

'Deep in the forest lies a lake, beautiful in its stillness. All around grow the stately trees of wisdom and the ground is carpeted with soft moss and flowers of every colour and perfume. The sun shines down caressingly upon this gentle scene and a soft breeze dances lightly among the leaves. Yet the surface of the lake remains undisturbed, a mirror of truth to all who have the courage to look; for he who would make a pilgrimage hither must come as a little child—naked yet unashamed—feet unshod, for here is holy ground. And when at last he kneels with humility before the mirror he will know himself—the evil that he has done and the good too, the hurts he has both given and received, and the degree of his love for self and others. And if, seeing, he accepts, and professes himself willing to learn the retribution of his faults, and humbly rejoices over any good which he has achieved, then will the trees of wisdom burst into flower, birds make sweet music, and the mirror of the lake smile upon the traveller. The gentle breeze will guide him again on his path and he will go in peace, patiently to learn all unto the end.

'But if, seeing, the pilgrim looks only for what he shall gain for himself, and not for the effect his living shall have had upon the world, then will the lake become troubled, the trees will droop and die, and the air will be angry with the beating of birds of prey; the silence shall be broken in a great storm, and this unhappy traveller shall be buffeted upon his path by a rude wind and shall suffer many things before he may again approach the hallowed spot.

'Learn that all experience is given not for the individual alone but for humanity.'

On the following day came another message:

'Deep within the mountain burns a fire, raging and relentless. Cast thyself into it; know the searing agony of its consuming heat; know sore humiliation as thou dost become as nothingness —dust to be wafted on any chance breeze; and know at last the rosy stillness, warmth, and peace to be found in the very centre of the roaring flames. Then shalt thou walk proudly forth, conqueror of the fire; and the fiery tongues shall recede from thy path and willingly obey thy every command.

'Know that the reward of all suffering is a measure of joy and peace, heaped up and running over. Fear not, weary pilgrim; the end is nigh and all is well.'

All this time we were still climbing the black mountain. A few days later came a third message:

'Deep in the waters lies a temple of stillness, *doré dedans et dehors*; it is a place of beauty and love. As the pilgrim floats through the gentle waters he is aware first of a world of shining gems in rich flashing colours, then all turns to silver and finally to the warmth and purity of gold. He who would come hither must clothe himself in white robes and he must be firmly dedicated to the Way. Here will much be received but much required, and all must be given in gladness and serenity of heart.

'This beauteous place marks no end to suffering but rather a beginning; he who comes will have trodden already a hard and testing path, and here is the place of decision. Strength, love, peace, are here in abundance, but descend not to these depths unless thy will and purpose are directed toward the light unto the end of thy days. Here, child, is the point of no return; if thou wouldst rest from thy labours, go in blessing and peace, and dwell in love and harmony in that quiet wood with thy husband and children. Bravely hast thou fought and suffered and joy is thy reward.

'If, though, thou canst suffer and labour more, and thou feelest thy spirit strong, then descend, child, descend to this temple, and take upon thee the charge to labour and suffer all that is required of thee, without complaint or question until the day of thy reward shall come.

'Meditate well, thou dearly beloved, the choice is of the gravest.'

In the inner world we continued climbing, and by July 17th we had reached the mountain top. It was a volcano, black, with nothing growing at all. Gildas said I must let go and drop into the crater—into the fire. During meditation with Mary I did so.

It felt both worse and better; worse in that I had left Gildas and the baby at the top and I disliked the separation; better because at last I had made the choice and was no longer hovering on the brink. Yet I felt that the process was only partly over.

Throughout the following four days I was steadily being burned up. There was less and less of me; all the time I was growing smaller.

On Sunday, July 23rd, came a tremendous experience which started precisely at 7.20 p.m., with a terrible dazed feeling. I noted the time as I was about to return home by scooter after a week-end away. Thinking the feeling would pass, I set out quite happily. However, the sensation grew worse and worse—I didn't know where I was—I could hardly remember where I was going, let alone which places to go through to get there. I was not aware of any phantasy, either in the inner world or on the other level—only this awful feeling of knowing nothing. The familiar journey became a nightmare of uncertainty; names on signposts might have been written in Russian for all they conveyed to me, and once I was hopelessly lost, right off the road I had travelled so many times. I was in despair, yet somehow, by the grace of some good influence, I *did* eventually arrive home; it was after midnight, and usually the journey took at the most three hours.

By the time I arrived it was obvious that something was happening of great importance, so I took off my outdoor things, wrapped myself in a blanket and, sitting on a chair, let it all come.

First came the pain. It had been with me all the time, but now it mounted to a great crescendo until I felt I could bear no more. I am not afraid of pain but I would have done anything to escape from this at its climax; to be alone somewhere where I could have screamed would have helped, but I dared not risk waking my landlady, who would hardly have understood! (For a while, though, I seriously contemplated asking her to send for a doctor as I was temporarily convinced that this was physical in origin after all.) Then quite suddenly, at the very end of my endurance, I relaxed; the pain surged around me but it was no longer my master, and slowly it subsided leaving me quiet and untormented.

The quietness was short-lived for now I was plunged into the inner world, right into the heart of the mountain of fire and its raging furnaces, 'deep within the mountain'. The inner pain followed much the same pattern as the outer. I suffered the 'scaring agony' and all the 'sore humiliation' as I was destroyed in the flames, reduced to 'dust to be wafted on any chance breeze'. Yet in this humiliation I knew many things I had come to the depths in order to learn (pray God I never forget). The shells broke and came away, and at the centre was a soft, vulnerable, sensitive creature, capable of giving and receiving the deepest love. I rejoiced and would have flung the shells far away, but then again I knew that this was wrong; the whole consisted of both shells *and* softness—both must be accepted, both allowed to play their parts. At last the eternal struggle of the two halves was resolved.

Now, as with the physical pain, the flames ceased to possess me. I came together and was able to stand up and 'walk proudly forth, conqueror of the fire'.

Now the morning light was coming, the darkness was almost past, and with the dawn other things in my suffering were made clear and complete also.

The witch appeared in all her horror and was slowly transformed into a beautiful statue of purest white, with flowing lines which seemed to link earth with heaven.

The black liquid welled up in all its evilness, then changed to the terrifying red sea, then to a milky fluid, and finally to clear water; and now there was a spring (flowing from a rock) from which flowed silver water, and at its source bloomed a beautiful golden flower.

> 'Not for ever by still waters
> Would we idly rest and stay,
> But would smite the living fountains
> From the rocks along our way.'

So the long night ended and day came once more. In the morning light I sat exhausted, but filled with serenity, thankfulness and praise.

Now Gildas brought me to a quiet place, and beautiful.

'Rest, my love, the suffering is over but you are far spent. This is like the point in an illness when healing is assured but there is still far to go in convalescence. You may feel strong and light, but be still within, my dear; this has taken much from you. It may be days before you are truly well and strong again—be patient, dear heart.

'As you grow stronger, though, there is still one thing to do: meditate upon the third message. It came to you rather early, but now is the time for meditation and decision. Do not rush; there is plenty of time.'

The Dedication

A month later, in meditation I was sitting peacefully beside the waters, pondering upon the decision which I must make; I had no idea which way to go, and during almost a week of frequent meditation it had been so. Yet I was not anxious or troubled for I knew that when the time came I should know what to do.

In imagination I made a choice (the choice of the ego). I left the still waters, turned my back upon them and found the quiet wood, my husband and children. All was bliss and peace. Then in my mind I heard that lovely voice with its gentle note of pleading: 'Descend, child, descend to this temple,' and then I knew which way I must take for peace of mind: my way led downwards to the temple and whatever else lay beyond.

After making this decision (or rather, knowing it), I went for a walk by the river and was deeply troubled; this was not what I *wanted* at all. There was still a weariness in me from my recent journey; I wanted to pass the rest of my days in quietness and peace. I rebelled against the Deep Centre which knew the way. Then I stopped, and it seemed as though a wreath of mist came from the river (though it was midday) and wrapped itself about me. And within the mist was a light, soft and radiant. My whole being was uplifted in worship, and all was beauty. Then the rebellious ego seemed to be melted gently away and I experienced that 'one-ness' as at Darwen Tower one winter. When the experience passed (I lost all sense of time so do not know how long it lasted), there was no rebellion in me, and I knew with every bit of me that the decision to descend was right; I was to 'clothe (myself) in white robes', to 'be firmly dedicated to the Way', and to 'take upon me the charge to labour and suffer all that is required . . . without complaint or question'.

I sat down near the river, wholly at peace. Suddenly a presence was with me, and that same gentle voice which had given the three messages spoke to me :

'Bravely hast thou chosen, my child. Yet seven days more shalt thou have in which to prepare and be sure. In prayer and meditation and fasting shall be thy preparation. Pray and meditate each day, and for seven days eat only fresh fruit and vegetables, and drink only milk or fruit juice. A little wholemeal bread and honey are also permissible. Be sure to wash well thy hands before eating; and each day take a relaxing bath in scented water. After seven days descend with thy Guide to the temple of stillness, if thou art ever steadfast in thy purpose. My blessing goes with thee.'

On Sunday September 3rd about 5 a.m., I stood with Gildas beside the waters and knew that the time had come to descend. 'Deep in the waters lies a temple of stillness'. Gildas was clothed in dazzling white with unshod feet, but I wore a long pale blue gown and sandals. Gently Gildas bent down and unfastened my sandals and gave me a pure white robe to wear in place of the blue one. Then, hand in hand, we slipped into the water and the message came alive :

'As the pilgrim floats through the gentle waters he is aware first of a world of shining gems in rich flashing colours, then all turns to silver, and finally to the warmth and purity of gold.'

At last, in a golden world we touched the bottom and there before us stood the golden temple of stillness. Its beauty is impossible to describe, but its stillness and 'goldenness' seemed to envelope us, and we became filled with peace and light.

Slowly we approached the temple gateway, and there we were met by a man whose face was old, wise and beautiful; his bearing was majestic, his presence at once awe-inspiring and comforting. He wore a robe which glowed and shimmered, continually giving out light and colour. I felt strengthened and uplifted, yet I knew that here was one who could see to the very depths of my being. When this marvellous person spoke, I could sense, too, his great love and compassion, and I knew his voice for that which had given the messages.

Now he questioned me, firmly but gently, and, kneeling before him, I knew what I must answer, as though following some formula.

'Child, what is thy purpose in coming hither? What dost thou seek to gain? What is thy True Name? And who is thy companion?'

'I come to dedicate my all in the service of the Light; I seek only to give and not to gain; my True Name and the name by which I am known are one, I am Ruth; my companion is my true love, my husband and Guide.'

'Dost thou come, Ruth, of thine own free will or at the persuasion of another?'

'I come of my own free will, persuaded by none.'

Then he turned to Gildas.

'Dost thou bring this child only to the temple threshold or wilt thou cross it with her? Wilt thou go wherever she doth go and guide her unto the end, or wilt thou give her now into the care of another?'

'This is my dearly beloved wife, whom I will never foresake. I will go wherever she doth go and guide her unto the end; her care is my concern, and she shall not be guided by another.'

'Both have answered well; enter now this place of peace.'

Then we were led into the temple; again the beauty which confronted us is indescribable; but there was an air of timelessness and serenity and I felt my whole being absorbed in stillness. The chamber we entered was circular, and in the middle was a smaller circular sanctuary, the doors of which were closed. In the chamber where we were the air was sweet with perfume, and quiet but beautiful music was all around. Surrounding the chamber were small alcoves, and the 'message-giver' took us into one of these. When we had sat down opposite him, he took my hands in his and began to talk.

'Ruth, my name is Naphat, and I am thy Great Teacher. Gildas is thy Guide and teacher too, and will always be with thee. I cannot be always with thee, and thou wilt not always need me, but when thou dost, I am here and will always come to thee if thou canst not come to me. My child, thou hast led black and evil lives long ago, and thou didst grow strong in wickedness. When at last thou turnedst to the Light, thy strength remained with thee to be used in better ways. Because thou art strong much is required of thee and thou hast much to suffer. Yet all who come here know for ever that with suffering goes much joy. We do not wish to stress the pain too much, but thou must know that thou wilt be tried according to thy strength. We warn thee of these things for we would not have thee turn from the path later, yet in warning we lose many; but thou, Ruth, remain steadfast to thy purpose, for thou art greatly loved and we have need of thy strength.'

'I am not worthy of your love and regard, Naphat, but I will remain steadfast in my purpose, and my love, my life, and my strength are dedicated to the Way of Light for ever.'

'My child, thou wilt often regret this day, and many temptations will beset thee, but they who make this dedication are greatly blessed and protected. There lies ahead a great task for thine undertaking; but now thou wilt be disappointed I fear, for it is not today that thou shalt be given the task; instead I give thee one which thou mayst think dull—but beware, because it is both harder and greater than thou thinkest. Go home, Ruth, to thy mortal husband, love him well and create a home where the atmosphere is one of peace and beauty. And now let us go into the inner sanctuary to meditate a while together. There, in the silence, Ruth, thou mayst make thy dedication and there shall be great rejoicing that yet another has joined those who strive to lighten the darkness.'

Then we went into the inner sanctuary, where all was silent, no music or perfume in the air, but a great and holy stillness. The experience within this sanctuary was like nothing I have ever thought or even dreamed about, too precious and wonderful to attempt to describe.

Of the return I remember nothing, as for many days I seemed to be surrounded with the beauty of the inner sanctuary, the goldenness of the temple, and the wonder of my experience.

CHAPTER 10

The Fourth Journey

September 1962 to April 1963

My marriage in the outer world was followed by a year's rest from inner journeys.

Mary was staying with me for a week-end when, as has been told in *Gildas Communicates*, on September 1st 1962, Gildas began to give teachings.

'This meeting has been planned, Ruth, between you and Mary, and has every blessing from the other side. The influence radiating outwards from this week-end may reach further than either of you can possibly conceive.'

At the same time he warned me :

'The Fourth Journey is near, my child; I had not thought it would be so, but even in the inner world we make mistakes and wrong calculations. Again, all that you do in these journeys concerns not only you but others in a much wider field—in a way which you will one day understand, but for now you must trust me that this is so.

'You are stronger, Ruth, than you feel. The main preparation must be in overcoming your fear, in meditation, in quietness, and in the establishment of a new mature trust in me. Mary will be your main help as you journey. She will know what to do and how to help when the time comes. I have told you before that you have passed the most painful journey; the others may seem harder in many ways but you will not find them so full of pain as the Third Journey. There is a great blackness which you must face, connected with things you have done in past lives, and there is some danger to yourself in undertaking this journey, but you have given yourself to be used for the light and you are to be used. I shall be with you, my dear, and you know you will come through safely. I cannot tell you the exact hour or any more at present, but you will be strengthened in Love and Light, as you know, and all will be well.'

In the night of September 3rd Gildas came to me and told me that we were now required to set out. He fastened a very fine gold chain round my right wrist and the other end he fastened to a marvellous brooch which he appeared to be wearing over his heart. The brooch was of gold and set with amber stones (the colour of the jewel), and in the centre was the hexagon.

'Now, my child, you are free to move at will; you will not find that this chain restricts you, but it is of a very great strength and cannot be broken; you have only to touch it with your left hand and through it you will receive strength and light from me and all who surround you in love and light upon this journey. I go with you, but you must be free for I cannot fight for you. This chain both leaves you free and yet joined to me. And now together we will go forward into the long night of strife and darkness. All I have, and can command, goes with you for ever.'

There seemed to be three levels of experience, all co-existent, first one being more sharply defined and then another, but all continuing without a break.

(1) After fastening the golden chain, I found myself sinking with Gildas in a black sea. I was naked, save for the jewel, strung as always round my waist. Gildas wore a robe of some kind but I was aware only of his marvellous brooch (to which my chain was attached) glowing brilliantly in the otherwise all-encompassing blackness. And so we drifted ever downwards; anxiety, depression and despair closed in upon me, and I wept as we went.

(2) A phantasy attributed by Gildas to the 'outer parallel' of the journey continued: six black figures relentlessly digging into my heart, and I unable or unwilling to fight against them.

(3) Of this third thing I can hardly bring myself to write, so horrid is it. I lie naked on a crude altar, my lips red and the taste of blood in my throat, indulging in crude sexual rites and perversions with a creature masked and horned in imitation of the devil. Part of me, looking down on this, is sickened and horrified, yet the part of me indulging in this thing is exhilarated and frenzied, intent on acquiring occult power to be used for base and selfish ends. All around are other frenzied figures, engaged in a nauseating orgy.

A fortnight later I contacted Gildas and asked him why I was feeling so 'stuck', why the journey was not progressing, and to help with the sexual side of the horrid vision of 'black magic' I had seen. He was full of strength, love, and compassion.

'My dearest child, what unnecessary sufferings you make yourself. Have you yet not enough trust and faith to know that when I have told you all will be well, it *will* be so? You have got into a distressed condition about this vision of a past life; you have used valuable strength regretting and agonizing over that which has gone and cannot be changed. You ask why you feel 'stuck'; is it not through your own foolishness that you are unable to go forward? These things are shown to you that you may learn from them. This vision is shown to you that you might know some of the reasons for the sufferings you are about to face. You did very wrong things in the past, some far worse than implied in that brief vision, but have I not told you before that your feet are on the True Path? Yet you will not be much helped by the negative attitude you have so far assumed; rather must you take note of the vision, repent of your evil past, but determine to go forward and learn the ways in which you may begin your atonement. The block is in yourself, my dear; in all else the time is ready for progression.

'As for the sexual side, what bothers you here? You misused creative energy—but already in this life you have suffered regarding sex, and come through. There were outer reasons for your sexual repression, of course, but here is the deeper reason which before you were not ready to be shown. Yet now you have made good sexual relationships, both inner and outer, and from such relationships—when the creative act is used with joy, wonder and spiritual as well as sensual pleasure—comes much light and life to be spread around.

'This much you have redeemed. Be not ashamed, my Ruth; be only determined never to be persuaded to abuse the great gift of sexual power in the like manner again. You have progressed far since that dark life, and severe would be the karma you would call upon yourself should you be tempted to fall once more. This is a grave warning, and one which you will later have cause to recall. Put all your mind and strength to holding your feet to the Path. You have been granted Initiation; the penalty of failure is great.'

I asked him, too, about receiving teachings. Mary had sent questions for Gildas to answer; how could I take teachings when I seemed absorbed in darkness and the demands of the journey?

'You must understand that there are many levels of consciousness and being. Though it may seem to you that you are wholly absorbed in darkness, in reality this is far from the truth. There are levels of consciousness to which you can aspire where this blackness does not exist. After the journey is over I will teach you how to contact these levels at will, and you will be able to use this knowledge to ease the strain of the two final journeys, for as you progress so is more help given to you. For now, since it is essential that the teaching should continue, I will use my power to lift you above your trials to a level where we may communicate and concentrate to the full.'

Gildas fulfilled his promise. It seemed as though I were taken up to a place of light and peace on a great spiral, and that while the teaching was given I rested in a warm embrace which gave me strength and vitality. Then, as the teaching ended, I descended to the darkness once more and there was a great weariness upon me. I felt used, emptied, yet satisfied, and the weariness was pleasant and relaxed. For a time all tension was gone, and I knew that the journey would progress at last.

In dreams, the phantasy of descending through dark water with Gildas continued. We went on and on downwards and it became ever blacker at each level. Then the descent became more and more difficult, as the water turned to slime and then to thick, foul filth (far worse than the most horrid mud), and through this we have literally to burrow our way. It is more than terrible, my every longing urges me to climb, and yet I must descend through a horror like this. Always before, the descent has been effortless (or seemingly so in comparison with this). I am overwhelmed, yet must go on.

The other phantasy changed a little, too. Now the black figures are distributed, one only digs into my heart, the rest dig deeply into other parts of my body. I feel no pain, yet I am trapped, heavy, unresistant, and so cold.

As for this 'third thing', considering all that Gildas had said, I had been trying to put it away from me, yet could not. Finally, while alone, I broke down and wept and wept as I have never wept before, and afterwards I could see that it was something which I could not step back and alter, but only redeem. I accepted it into myself, as part of my pattern, and instead of resenting having been shown this vision, gave thanks that I was permitted to see even a little of the meaning and reason behind my life or lives.

Aspects and Levels of Experience

What do I feel? Where am I? What am I? What is my suffering? What is this strong correlation between these inner journeys and my personal psychology? In the intervals between journeys I am clear-headed, I have direction, I am 'normal'—just an ordinary, every-day person weaving my pattern through life. I have my ups and downs, like others, but it is all acceptable, all natural; this *is* life. I have, too, my own 'inner life'—my sanctuary of peace—to which I may withdraw at will and draw strength for living, but this too is me, and, I have come to realize, natural and normal in persons of my 'type'. To those who understand, this 'inner life' may be communicated; to those with whom it would be impossible to share this thing I show my ordinary outer self and am (mostly) content. Both worlds are real, and in both I live and am and have my being. Yet when a journey is upon me, only the inner things are real, black though they may be, and the outer world becomes a place with which I cannot identify. I must needs attend to certain tasks in order to maintain my own well-being and that of others to whom I am committed, but it is irksome, there is no joy, no fulfilment herein; I only long to be free, unfettered, to withdraw and to work upon the 'inner things'.

Then, too, these inner things exist on different levels: at one I perform them with love, as a task to which I am committed which involves not only 'me' but humanity.

At another, they are 'real', and I am deeply involved; they are pain and humiliation, or peace and ecstacy, and I feel it all and am moved and taught by my feeling.

Again, they are purely psychological—especially the suffering —and need interpretation and application to unresolved conflicts, unaccepted behaviour, which go to make up the 'me' who lives today.

Then, my Guide speaks to me of karma, and yet another level is found—and all these things are separate and yet mysteriously bound in one.

Now I am heavy, cold, and slow. What do the inner symbols mean to me? What are the lessons I am now to learn? The filth on the level of karma I understand, but on the personal level— no.

And what is this digging into me? I am at sea completely here, can hardly begin to find the real significance which will set me free. The pattern is always the same: once I recognize the truth behind the symbols I am free, and the phantasies no longer recur. I feel a need to write it all out, and perhaps clues will emerge from the writing.

I am so cold tonight and cannot, even by the fire, get warm. The experience of digging through the filth grows close about me —I can feel it—cold and clammy—it chills my spine; it is foul, suffocating, and now it begins to heave, moved no doubt by some evil force. It churns upwards and I must go downwards . . .

A fortnight passed.

The filth was seething now, and I had to go on ever downwards. I was truly in despair and hardly knew how to go on; progress was dreadfully slow and every inch gained was a major battle. As I 'worked' on this is quietness, the despair deepened until it became an agony; this was a dark and drear moment in

time when I was exhausted and without hope. Then suddenly
it seemed as if from some dark recess of the experience there was
a thought, a memory, which held out hope and light in this
otherwise grim moment. Slowly the memory became accessible,
and I reached at last for the golden chain—that link which
Gildas had promised would bring light and power. As always,
his promise was fulfilled. As I touched the chain I felt (though
I did not see) his marvellous presence and power surrounding
me amidst all the horror. I was renewed, and knew that I could
now go on—and on I went, deeper and ever deeper into the
seething mass, but now I was strong, and able to bear this thing,
to go through it to whatever might lie beyond. I was surrounded,
and to some extent lifted above and beyond the experience, by a
marvellous love and presence. As I went deeper, the filth became less 'solid', but was packed with all manner of horrid
creeping and slimy creatures. Just previously to the 'renewing',
this would have daunted me entirely; I should have gone back,
given up, endeavoured to go back on my initiation—anything
rather than face this additional horror; but now I went on with
a new determination, knowing that, with perseverance and
acceptance, this thing will pass.

[As in the Third Journey, here I had reached a point at which
I could no longer write up the journey, stage by stage; the
suffering, exhaustion, and cold were too great. The rest, therefore, was written after it was over, mostly in August 1963. These
experiences went on continuously from October 1962 to April
1963.]

Gradually now, after the experience of renewal, my new
determination enabled me in some way to become master of
the slime and filth and creeping creatures. I began to observe
them with detachment, and, as this change in me took place, so
the creatures became less, the mud changed to water, and at
last I began to float downwards instead of having to fight every
inch of the way.

Now I came into a cool green world; Gildas was near and for
a time I knew peace. This was a world of green, translucent
beauty, supremely restful, and new strength flowed into the
fibres of my soul. I felt calm and strong, ready for all, but here

was only a lull before the storm, and it was well that in this brief tranquillity I knew not what lay ahead.

The Weeds and the Green Sea-Witch

All too soon, it seemed, the moment came to continue, and as I set forth, walking now along the water's bed, I came gradually into a dense forest of terrible weeds. These plants seemed to be more than plants and to have a will of their own. As I tried to pass, they clung to me and held me, choking me and giving me a feeling of suffocation. They were tough and sinuous and almost impossible to break. The only sure way of releasing their hold was to tug them up by the roots, and this took great strength. While I was coping with one weed, others grew rapidly around me, holding me in tight bondage, sapping all my strength. Each step forward demanded the utmost vitality, and I wept with exhaustion and desperation. Yet once again, as I reached this point of despair, I was helped; with a new lease of strength I pulled at the roots of those plants with the thickest and most strangling tentacles, and at last reached clear water once more.

The surge of spirits which accompanied this escape was short-lived, for the next obstacle lay immediately before me—or rather rose up grotesquely in my path. A great green sea-witch barred my way, and physical strength was of no use at all. I quailed before the magical gaze of this fascinating creature. She stared upon me, and forward I could not go. Slowly, at the insistence of her will I moved backwards, once again, into the horrid clutches of the weeds. In misery and pain I fought my way free once more but still I had not the strength to withstand the gaze of the magical witch, and three times in all I returned to the horrible world of the weeds.

At last I was given strength to resist the witch's gaze; I kept my eyes from meeting hers and moved slowly away from her lair. Each step was agony and I hoped, in part, to succumb to her spell, and go back and live a pale, enclosed life, choked for ever by the weeds around the witch's lair. Yet that part of me which knows these things took supreme command and I achieved the journey past the witch—and, as I passed, the most awful scene and ordeal were enacted. The great witch of the sea crumpled and shrivelled like a dead flower and, screaming and giving forth a stream of meaningless curses, she died in agony, polluting the sea with a cloudy, acrid, stinging substance; yet the feel of this upon my skin was as nothing to the inner turmoil and agony aroused by this death. The death of the sea-witch was as painful to me as to her, and I too longed for death or oblivion. I felt as though every part of me, both inner and outer, had been scraped raw, and that I was left alone, helpless, and without hope of healing.

Almost blindly, in a world of utmost pain, I stumbled on, yet as I went I felt a newness and a softness filling my body, and the healing which it had seemed hopeless to wish for began to take place, though I was still terribly unhappy and depressed.

Now I reached a long straight road, and went on and on. It was desolate and uninteresting and I was wretched in the extreme. The road seemed to have no end; the situation seemed unbearable, yet I knew I must plod wearily on. (There was an interesting parallel in the outer world, for about this time I drove through Norfolk, and the intermingling of inner and outer was terrible; there was no chance of even momentary escape; the drive seemed endless, and on arrival I felt dreadfully tired and ill, though I recovered fairly quickly.)

Now Mary reminded me of the golden chain which Gildas said I only needed to touch in order to gain help and strength. I had completely forgotten this, but when I touched it Gildas was immediately very close to me, and instead of being able only to feel his presence, now I could see him and walk within the aura of light which he always radiates. Again in my utmost despair help had come to sustain and comfort me. Now, too, I was terribly cold within and without; in the bitter weather of this winter it seemed impossible to get warm.

The Cavern of Gold and the Sarcophagus

Fortunately, after what seemed an endless time, the long straight road ended quite suddenly, and we dropped down over a sheer cliff side. At first we fell through space, and then we seemed to be going down through a narrow shaft. At last we landed on a narrow rock-strewn ledge, with a tremendous drop below it. Gildas leading, we made an extremely perilous journey and came eventually to a great cavern lined with gold; yet what might have been a place of richness, light and beauty seemed eerie and sinister. This gold gave forth no light or lustre, and I had no feelings of finding something precious (as on my first journey). I felt apprehensive and still so dreadfully cold. Then Gildas led me to a plain stone door and bade me enter, which I did, and found myself in a stone tomb or sarcophagus cut exactly to my shape. With a gentle yet unsmiling glance, Gildas closed the door, so that he was without and I within, yet I felt now the strong link of the chain which joined us, and could feel his presence and love surrounding me in this dreadful place.

This was the beginning of a period of extreme mental anguish and trial. Strange visions and thoughts were with me and round me, and I began a terrible mental battle with some evil force. It was horrible and exhausting, and I was desperately in need of the sustaining thoughts and prayers of my friends. (I was terribly alone, and as the time went on and the struggle continued I sorely missed the direct therapeutic help from Mary which had made the other journeys so much lighter in comparison. I found I could not even communicate by letter; false fears of being a 'nuisance' made me try to carry on without sharing my utmost misery and wretchedness, and I began to feel as though I just could not carry on—I should be ill both physically and mentally. Fortunately despair drove me to make contact, and with sympathy and understanding at the outer level I found at last the dregs of my courage and was able to hold on and continue.)

I moved around as though in a dream; days passed, yet I hardly seemed to know or keep count of the passage of outer time. The inner world was the only thing 'real', and how terrible a reality! At times pictures would appear in my inner consciousness; the forces of evil would invade my exhausted mind in the form of persuasive, kindly creatures endeavouring to appear as beings of Light. They would entice me with promises of wonderful rewards if only I would turn and follow once more the paths of darkness. Then the figures would become threatening, menacing, terrifying; facing them and endeavouring to remain calm was mental torture. Yet still worse were the times when no 'pictures' were there, and I was tortured with the feeling that evil forces were searching my mind with the intention of taking possession and using me for evil ends. And still my hell was not complete: I suffered an impelling temptation to do just what the evil ones were conspiring for. At times a large part of me *wanted* to follow the dark path, yet still I held to the golden chain of Gildas. The torment was indescribable, as though I could not survive this thing in one piece but should be rent in twain. (The digging experience still continued simultaneously on its own level.)

Slowly, however, relief, strength and confidence broke through into my inner confusion, and I began to realize that my love for Gildas, which held me to the True Path, was stronger than all things; that I should never forsake him, and that therefore the seemingly inconclusive battle was in all reality won—yet still the conflict had to be experienced and endured.

Soon after this realization, the temptation became less, and then I was able to say firmly to myself, 'I will *not* be invaded'. The unbearable tension began at last to lessen, and finally the conflict reached a terrible and dramatic climax. In the night I awoke to find the room full of evil. I saw nothing but was aware of not being alone and that whatever presence was with me was powerful and black. A cold chill went right through me, and I knew real terror. Time ceased to exist, my mind went blank and I could not think or move or cry out. At last my brain began to function, but all I could think of was 'Gildas—Gildas!' and suddenly he was with me and everything was out of my hands. Gildas stood beside me, level with my head; I was still unable to move but knew he was standing very straight, staring ahead, and slowly he began to glow with a marvellous light. I was comforted, but the atmosphere of the room had not altered, and I could do nothing. I was like a dead log. Then, over and above me I saw the cross in a circle of light, protecting and encircling my whole body. Slowly I relaxed as the evil receded, and went almost immediately to sleep. In a dream I was plunged deep into the inner world and the sarcophagus. There I was aware that the evil forces with which I had fought for so long were directed towards endeavouring to break the chain which linked me with

Gildas. At first I was afraid that they would succeed, but suddenly my faith returned. Gildas had said that the chain, though fine, was unbreakable, and I recognized that these evil forces themselves realized that the battle was over. They were making one last ludicrous attempt at success, and I laughed aloud with the release from tension which this realization brought. There was a horrid sound, like a screech, wail and moan joined into one, and for a moment my terror returned, but then I knew it was the death cry of all I had been fighting and that the battle was over.

The sarcophagus opened and I was gently helped free by Gildas. How different was the gold-lined cavern! Now the precious metal gave forth its true light and lustre and was beautiful to behold. My heart rejoiced that the evil had departed, and that now, here, deep down among the dark places of the inner world, was a cavern—an oasis—of light.

I was weak and could hardly stand but for the support of Gildas. Now he lifted me gently in his arms and carried me, kissing my lips and whispering tender words in my ear. Then he laid me gently down, still in the cavern of gold, on his own soft cloak and said,

'Rest, my love, and I will watch awhile; we have yet further to go, though the darkest time is past. But now you are weak and weary; rest, and while you sleep my love shall revive and strengthen you and you will be enabled to continue. Have no fear, I am ever beside you.'

And so I slept, thankfulness and peace in my heart, cared for by my beloved Gildas, and secure in the knowledge that surely all would be well.

I remained resting in the cavern of gold for quite a long time. At first I was hardly aware of anything except the marvellous love and the healing of Gildas. I was terribly weak, and my strength returned so very slowly. Although Gildas can heal to some extent, and his love is a kind of healing in itself, he is not a Healer in the sense of being dedicated to this work, so I was visited and given strength and a kind of virtue by the marvellous presence of Sylvan the Blue, one of the Great Healers, until I was ready to continue the journey.

Return to the Light

After a while, I *was* very much stronger and felt able to continue; we set out, Gildas and I, for the journey back to the Light. We left the cavern of gold and journeyed on through other caverns. The way was dark, but Gildas was beside me and I knew that we were going upwards and that every step was taking us nearer to the Light and the end of the journey. There were no more trials now, just a steady upward plodding towards the joy of another journey accomplished.

After some time we emerged from the caverns and walked along a narrow ledge with a sheer drop to the right of us, but I was not afraid now, and still the path led upwards, and already it was beginning to seem lighter. This was comparatively easy after the desperate rigours of the earlier part, but despite the marvellous healing I was easily tired, and soon I was quite faint with exhaustion. Yet we had to go onwards; there was no resting place on this narrow ledge.

Suddenly the ledge came to an end and we were faced by a sheer cliff or rock. I was thrust into despair, for I knew we must climb this cliff face, yet even as the despair enveloped me, it became quite light all around us, and Gildas touched my hand and said.

'This is the last obstacle in our path, my dear. Call with all your remaining strength for help; do not allow yourself to be defeated now; the end is immediately before us.'

These words steadied me. I asked as hard as I could for help as we began the perilous ascent. Footholds and fingerholds were rare; there were no ledges to rest on. I was already desperately weary, and I knew not what it was that pushed me ever upwards. Often I stumbled or slipped and would have crashed down to the depths but for the alertness of Gildas, who would give me his hand. His touch was bliss to my torn and bleeding fingers, and each time gave me the strength to renew my efforts.

At length we reached the top, and, pulling myself over the edge of the precipice into the Light, I sank utterly exhausted upon the soft, scented grass, while healing, cleansing breezes fluttered gently about me. Wearily I smiled at Gildas, who took me gently in his arms and carried me, as I fell into a deep, refreshing sleep, to the wonderful Sanctuary of Healing of Sylvan the Blue. Here all was beauty and light and peace; gradually I was healed and cleansed and refreshed, until the nightmare journey took on its right perspective, and I could look back with joy and thankfulness that yet another trial was over.

CHAPTER 11

The Fifth Journey

September to November 1963

On September 7th, in meditation, I was lifted into realms of light and peace and joy, and felt around me the wonderful presence of my Great Teacher, who spoke to me, beginning with the word he had used in other messages to me :

'Deep beneath the waters, deep beneath the fire, the darkness, the suffering, and the tribulation lies a place of exquisite Light and Healing. Here are brought poor souls who through their own or others' misdeeds have forgotten what it is to walk in light or to know peace of mind, and who must be given a special kind of strength and virtue before they will be able to turn from their evil and dark paths, begin to redeem their heavy karma, and tread the paths of light and love and righteousness. These souls grow not strong in the evil paths they tread; always they are weak and used by those of stronger will and evil power, and when they show the smallest spark of repentance they must be brought to this special place until that spark, with love, shall be nurtured and fanned into a flame which will grow steadily stronger and light their way to redemption.

'To this place, my child, thou must journey, and this shall be the Fifth Journey which thou must make. Thou art being given chance to redeem some heavy karma, for in thy distant evil past thou didst take and destroy one of those poor souls in pursuit of thine own ends, and he has never had the strength to lift himself from the mire into which thou wast the first to cast him. He has suffered much, but always when he returns to earth he is led into evil ways, and cannot resist the temptation to follow the path which he ever hopes will give him sudden power. This soul we put into thy charge for the arduous journey to the place where he shall be healed. This task is difficult and painful for thee, my child, for thou wilt see this soul, not as a grown man, but as an ugly, deformed, dirty, unloveable child, whom thou must take with thee through places where thou wilt grow un-utterably weary and where thou wilt truly feel that thy God has forsaken thee. Yet through all this somehow thou must love and cherish the little creature in thy charge. If thou dost show fear, he will be frightened too and may try to break away from thee and be lost or harmed: thou must protect and fight for him as a mother would protect and fight for her only son.

'Gildas shall go with thee, but his lips shall be sealed, his presence thou mayst have for comfort, but his wisdom thou must learn not to rely upon, but rather to search deep within thyself for the right decisions in each difficulty upon the way.

'One more thing I must tell thee: thou and the child go forth alone in every way (apart from the presence of Gildas) and thou must tell no one in the outer world about this journey until it is over. Thou must be thine own strength, wisdom and comfort. If all goes well, this journey will not be very long; thou wilt be free to return near the end of the second month from this.

'My child, I see that this task lies heavily upon thee. If I could I would give to thee the robe of my wisdom and the shimmering cloak of my experience, yet the very possession of these has taught me that these valuable things cannot be given by another; only when woven by thyself dost thou learn the true value of this raiment, so go forth, my child, and remember that though thou dost seem alone, thou art a member of this group and light and strength shall surround thee as thou goest.'

* * * * *

[The rest was written after the journey had ended, as was promised, at the end of November.]

My Great Teacher left me, and I was alone in the lovely place of our meeting, yet though all about me was light and beauty, within I was plunged into the depths of despair and heaviness. I was filled with resentment and fought desperately against all that my Teacher had said. I seemed barely to have recovered from the Fourth Journey, yet now I was required to set out once again into the realms of darkness. This was my frame of mind when Gildas appeared bringing the waif whom I had to accompany to the place of healing and regeneration. Whilst listening to my Great Teacher, as he spoke of this 'lost soul', I had felt within me the spark of compassion for this being whom I, in my wicked past, had set upon the evil path and used for my own selfish ends. Yet when I looked at the deformed, filthy, evil-looking scrap with whom Gildas presented me, my heart became as hard as stone. Hatred, anger, resentment flared up to such a degree that I could hardly contain them, yet from somewhere I knew I must find enough 'caring' to take this creature safely to his destination. My being seemed torn in two: on the one side a wise, patiently reasoning 'me' dedicated to follow the Path and to do my utmost to achieve any task given to me, and on the other the hard, ruthless person who wished only to be left alone, to be allowed to forget the past and drift through life just 'getting by'—this latter self was the one filled with hatred and anger at the task before me, and its emotions were by far the more real and compelling.

I was appalled at the filthy state of this child. He was literally black with ingrained filth; his hair was long and matted, and the lower part of his scantily covered body was encrusted with his own excrements. Worst of all, the child was little more than a baby and Gildas was carrying him in his arms and I realized that throughout the journey ahead I should have to carry this loathsome bundle for most of the time. Gildas gently put the child in my arms, though I almost recoiled in horror, and could not meet the gaze of my dear but silent Guide.

Since I now realized I would have to carry the child, and not from any concern for the child himself, I was determined not to set out upon the journey until he was cleaner. Gildas obviously read my intent and led me to a place where there lay a clear pool, and here, forcing myself to muster as much gentleness as possible, I stripped off the filthy rags and rubbed and scrubbed until the child was a good deal cleaner; I washed, cut, and

combed his hair, then dressed him in a clean, soft garment supplied by Gildas. The child was improved, but it would have taken
weeks of care to remove all the grime from his body, and his
skin was still grey and hard, horny and repulsive to touch.

It now occurred to me that the child must be hungry, and I
wondered about food for him—not with real concern, but with
a resentful 'since this task is mine' attitude; but even as I
wondered about this problem I knew in my heart of hearts what
the answer must be. I found the idea which occurred to me so
utterly repulsive that I pushed it away, but always it returned,
until I knew I should have to act upon it, that it was in fact
what was required of me. There was milk in my breasts for this
creature for whom I could find not one spark of love or compassion. Almost overcome with nausea, I pulled the child to my
breast and performed what I felt to be an utterly revolting task.
When it was over—and it seemed to last for an eternity—I left
the child with Gildas, and went away and was violently sick;
then I returned and, lying near Gildas with the child between us,
I cried myself to sleep. (This nausea was so marked it showed
itself in the outer world and for two or three days I was unable
to take any solid food and felt utterly miserable and ill.)

When I awoke, a little refreshed and seeing things more coolly
and dispassionately, I realized the karmic justice behind this feeding of the child: as I once had, in a sense, fed on this soul, in
order to pursue my own evil ends, so now he had to feed from
me; but this realization didn't make this thing any easier to bear.
Soon the child and Gildas were awake, and again I cared for
and fed my charge, but I did so once more grudgingly and under
a heavy cloud of resentment and misery. The feeding process I
still found sickening and repulsive in the extreme. Soon after this
routine, we set out in earnest upon the journey, going, as always,
downwards. This time we were descending a cliff face, sheer and
dangerous, and I had the child to carry. I soon discovered that,
though apparently a baby, this creature had a will of its own, and
certainly wasn't co-operating in its journey to 'redemption'. I
wanted to carry it on my back in order to leave both my hands
free to cope with the descent, but this was impossible as the
child would not hold at all and seemed intent on causing himself

to drop into the great gorge below us. Somehow I held on to the struggling bundle and managed to achieve the comparative safety of a fairly wide ledge, where I sat for a while with Gildas to think and regain strength and courage for the next part of the descent. It was while sitting here that I hit on the idea for holding the child secure and also leaving my hands free. I tore a piece from the robe I was wearing and managed to fasten the child securely on my back, Indian fashion. As we continued our descent, I was able to go much faster, but the child screamed with rage and punched and kicked until I could have pulled him from my back and cast him down into the gorge myself.

When we left the top of the cliff it had been sunny and pleasantly warm, but as we descended it became darker and hotter. The heat was now becoming intense and only just bearable. Then in the gathering gloom I found that we were descending into a thicket which seemed to be growing on the cliff face. I descended a little further but the thicket became more dense, and now there were thorn bushes with enormous thorns which tore painfully at my flesh. The child too was getting quite a share of jabs from the thorns; this fact didn't really worry me for I had no feelings except those of hatred and resentment for the pathetic little being, but then a look from Gildas reminded me that this soul was in my charge and the object of the Fifth Journey was to deliver him safely to the place of his redemption. I was obliged to untie the child and carry him high on my shoulders above the thorns, but he didn't struggle now as I think he was afraid of falling head first into the thorny mass. We went on for only a few steps more and I began to realize that we seemed to have reached an impasse. I tried uprooting some of the thorns (which were unbelievably tough) and got dreadfully scratched in so doing. To make matters worse, two or three other bushes immediately sprang up where the one had been. Now I sensed that this was not something through which I had to fight and force a way, as on other journeys, and with other obstacles, so I stood quietly and began to think what significance the thorns could have. Soon I understood that the thorns were there preventing progress on this journey as a symbol of my hatred and resentment and all the other negative feelings which were welling up within me. Each journey, I knew, must be accepted at a basic level, and undergone with a certain kind of love and devotion—and this I did not seem able to do at this time. I was fighting every inch of the way—not for progress upon the journey but against the fact that I should have to make this attempt or perform this task. Yet even as I realized this, I asked myself in anger and despiar, how *can* I bring myself to an acceptance of this task? How can I undertake a journey through dark places with this repulsive bundle for whom my only feeling is hatred? How can I care for him and protect him with what should amount to love and compassion, when my heart feels as heavy and as hard as stone? My mental anguish was great, and Gildas came quietly behind me and took the child gently away, then left me alone for a while among these thorns of my own making. I looked down at my body; I was covered in blood and still bleeding profusely from the wounds of my thorny barrier; I sank to the ground in despair, hardly feeling the physical pain from the pricks of my thorny bed, in this moment of mental torment. I began to cry, bitterly and in anguish, and as I wiped the tears away I saw that they were tears of blood.

Bathed in my own blood, I gradually became calmer and began to see clearly again. I had a vivid picture of my initiation in the temple 'deep beneath the waters', and of how there I had been so sure that I could accept and suffer and make the best of any task given to me, and I asked myself, 'Are you now rejecting your promises? Do the aims of which you were aware, and which you pledged so willingly to follow, no longer mean anything to you? Why are you so bitterly rejecting and resenting the law of karma? Why can't you regain that state of mind which would not show resentment, but gratitude at being allowed this chance to redeem some very dark karma?'

I could not fully answer these questions, but I realized that I needed help and prayed aloud that healing might be brought to the dark places of my mind which seemed to have gained control of me. Slowly, as I lay face down among the thorns, covered in blood, I felt a soft healing radiance pass over my body, gently caressing me, and resting finally and with great power over my head—then it was gone, but I felt at peace. Now as I thought about the journey ahead I still dreaded it, and at one level there was still resentment and hatred for my task, but deep within me the dedication which I had 're-lived' in my vision of my initiation remained alive, and there was a basic determination to win through at all events, which had not been there before. Deliberately I turned my thoughts to the child, my charge. Again, at one level there remained contempt and scorn for a soul so weak that he should sink so deep in mire and gain nothing from it. This part of me did not condemn him for following the paths of evil and darkness, but rather scorned him for having reaped nothing from his chosen way. Yet now, at a deeper level, there was compassion for this poor soul who had never really had a chance, and an understanding that since I had been the author of his downfall I must also help and save him. I felt shame for the weight of karma which I know I carry and joy and relief to know that I could now, with determination, do something to make the scales balance again.

Now I got up to look for Gildas and the child and saw, to my relief, that the thorns and thicket had completely vanished. Gildas, smiling, was bringing the child towards me. Looking at the little being I still felt revulsion, but clinging to that deeper feeling of compassion I took him and held him gently for a moment in my arms before Gildas helped me to tie him safely on my back once more, and we resumed our descent. As we went, it grew ever darker and hotter until I began to feel we must be descending into the very jaws of some mediaeval hell. We were nearing the bottom of the cliff now though, but soon I heard an ominous bubbling noise and we became surrounded by steam; a few more steps of descent, and there was a red, bubbling mass —red, boiling water—and the steam which surrounded us was excruciatingly hot; I could feel the exposed skin on my face and arms blistering in the heat.

The child, not unnaturally, was screaming and struggling; my first reaction was one of impatience, since I was suffering intense pain from the heat and blistering and was anxious about how we were to descend through these 'waters', but then deeper feelings took over, and, slipping him from my back, I tried to comfort him. Now a cool breeze began to blow and, taking advantage of this, I sat down and began to feed the child. Feeding him still made me feel sick and wretched, but basically I had *accepted* the justice of the karmic law, and this acceptance *did* make things a little easier.

As I finished feeding the child, I noticed to my horror that the boiling red mass was creeping nearer, and realized that something would have to be done about making a decision on how to overcome this obstacle. Since the cooling wind had now stopped and the pain from blistering caused by the steam was enough almost to drive me mad, and the red water was almost lapping round my toes, the decision had to be made quickly. I picked up the screaming, struggling child and spoke gently to him to soothe him so that his struggles should not add unnecessarily to my problems. Quickly I tied the child upon my back once more and, realizing that we could not go back, and that if we remained where we were we should be overcome by the boiling redness, I plunged desperately into the centre of it all, hardly waiting to see if Gildas was with us, yet knowing that he would never fail me. The breaking through the surface of the red water was excruciatingly painful; I thought I had made the wrong decision and that we should be destroyed in this terrible place. I screamed aloud in extreme agony of body and mind. Yet this moment of pain was not long and soon I realized that we had plunged into the centre of a whirlpool and now were being drawn steadily away from the foaming angry surface to the depths. As we descended, the heat became less so that it was uncomfortable, but not unbearable. I closed my eyes and let myself and the child be taken by the current. I relaxed and a deep peace was with me for this part of the descent, allaying my recent frantic fears, anxiety, and pain.

I entered into a state of dreaminess and, as we went ever downwards, sucked by the current through the red water, I gradually became aware of my surroundings or the passage of time, until suddenly I realized that the redness was no longer about me, and I was lying with the child beside me on a terrible stinking mass of decaying bones. Still the atmosphere seemed steamy and terribly hot and the smell from the mass of bones was indescribable. The child started to scream for attention, and too weary and sick at heart to protest much I fed him there and then in that awful place and bathed him with my tears. All the time Gildas was near in the background, and though he could give me no advice it was a great comfort to see him there. This place with the bones terrified me beyond all telling. I don't know *why* I was afraid, yet I was, though apart from being unpleasant there seemed nothing dangerous or frightening in the presence of the bones themselves. Yet now I was filled with a wild unreasoning unseeing panic and desire to be gone from this place. The child sensed the heat of my emotions and began to scream once more and struggle in my arms, as though he would break away from me and be gone. Now, at this unlikely moment, it seemed there was born in me the first spark of conscious compassion and tenderness for this poor deformed mite in my charge, and, soothing and calming him with gentle words and loving gestures, I forgot some of my own panic and began warily to go forward over the sharp uneven surface. My feet were bare and there were many sharp edges and pointed pieces of bone sticking out in different places and soon the soles of my feet were dreadfully cut and painful and bleeding. I could have stopped and torn strips from my robe to bandage them, but I was determined to leave this place of horror with all speed, and so I stumbled on. Now a hot mist descended and I could see only a few yards ahead of me. It was not possible to tell what lay ahead, as in my panic I had taken in nothing of the surrounding scene; all my being had been centred in dread upon those foul bones. Now I knew not which way I went, forward or back, or whether I trod an unending circle of agony and apprehension. Soothing the child helped me to keep control of myself and on I went, hoping and praying that my steps took me forward, and wishing desperately that Gildas who followed in my wake could have led me along the right path. Yet this was not to be, and soon from the steaming mist arose another horror. The bone-covered ground around me seemed to tremble, and through the mist huge terrifying shapes began to form themselves as though the bones were coming once more to life in the form of prehistoric animals—a whole army of tremendous ghastly skeletons.

This horror slowly took shape, and then, as though with one accord, these creatures turned and lumbered towards us. I was sickened and terrified and longed above all things to throw myself and the child into Gildas' arms and beg him to use his power to protect us; but I could not, for on this journey I must make the decisions alone, for myself and for the pathetic child whom I had been entrusted to carry through a difficult journey to the place where he would be redeemed. I knew that Gildas *would* help for, with his wonderful power, he would strengthen me in the decisions I must make, but there could be no sheltering from the storm in the circle of his arms, and since his lips were sealed, no comforting or strengthening word. A swift and painful memory came to me of another journey when I had encountered monsters like these, and when I had been trodden into the mire despite my struggles against them. I longed to turn back and run the way I had come, to endure the thorns or the hot red mass, *anything* rather than face this dreadful hazard, yet I knew that turning back would be of no avail, since, if this thing had to be faced, it would come sooner or later anyway, and flight would only postpone the dreaded moment. So, feeling sheer panic within, and clinging to the child as much for something to hold on to as for comfort for him, I stood as straight as I could and walked forward to meet the awful creatures who came ever towards me through the mist. I didn't know what to do, to face them and hope their ranks would part and allow me to pass, to fight them with all my strength, or to submit myself and allow them to do their worst. I chose the way which for me seemed the most difficult—submission. Whether the choice was right I did not know, but just prayed that I should not be allowed to stray from the way which I must follow. The creatures came on relentlessly, and, realizing we should be crushed beneath them, and with a new and real desire to protect the child in my charge, I put him on the putrefying ground and shielded him with my own body. There was a time when I knew the utmost agony, as if every bone in my body was shattered into many pieces as what seemed like an endless tribe of these great skeleton monsters pounded over us. I suppose I had hoped that the ground would 'give', and so it did, but not until I had experienced what seemed an eternity of excruciating agony. Suddenly there was relief, and clinging to the child I began to drop into darkness.

The fall was not long and we landed gently into a place where in a kind of dim half-light I could perceive a clear pool, and around it soft grass on which to rest. The child was sleeping now; I laid him on the grass and plunged myself into the clear water of the pool, and felt myself cleansed, refreshed and healed of my panic and pain. Now I woke the child; my mother-instinct seemed to be taking over my former revulsion, and I gently bathed him and washed his clothes. I myself had remained naked after my bathe, and when, as I rubbed the child dry with my own robe, he put up a hand and caressed my breast, I did not draw away but found the gesture pleasing and for the first time willingly, calmly and peacefully fed my charge. I looked down at him and noticed how he was changing; his skin was soft, smooth and pink, and he did not seem so ugly or deformed and out of proportion. When he had been fed his clothes were dry, and I dressed him and we settled down close together to sleep. Gildas was still near and he too slept near us and his presence comforted me.

When I awoke, the scene had changed to one of the utmost horror, and events followed which I can hardly bring myself to describe. I was still naked, and seemed at this time to be alone; I was not aware of the child or of Gildas but was transfixed with terror at what was happening. The cool clear water had gone from the pool, and there was a great pit of repulsive black slime; I was lying in slime and filth and could not move, I had to lie and let this horror happen. From the pit of slime came long slimy black snakes which made a devastating and terrible attack which I was powerless to prevent or attempt to fight. These snakes entered the lower part of my body and I could feel the sickening horror of them within me. They entwined themselves around my arms and legs and the outer part of my body, they were around my breasts and took the milk which I had only just learned to give willingly to the child. They entered my mouth and were entwined around my head and I was utterly nauseated and prayed for death, since I felt I would never be clean again.

Strangely enough, the child was my salvation. Suddenly he came, a golden flower in his hand, laughing and pink and loveable and these loathsome creatures of filth confronted with this childlike picture disappeared as suddenly as they had come and I was violently sick.

At last, utterly exhausted, I sank into a blissful unconsciousness, and when I felt consciousness returning, I struggled to remain in the dim world of unknowing. Slowly unwelcome awakening took possession of me and, as the painful memory of my experience returned, I felt a great hate and revulsion for my body; I was sure that I must be clothed in filth and would thus remain, rejected by all for ever. I looked down at myself; I was no longer lying in slime, but once more upon soft fragrant grass, and I was clothed in a clean garment of a lovely pale blue. Gildas lay near by, playing with the child who remained as I had last seen him, utterly transformed. I realized that we must go on and forced myself to look toward the spot whence the snakes had come. The scene had changed again and now was a great pit of fire, into which I realized we must fling ourselves to descend still further. At the outset of this journey my Great Teacher had said, 'Deep beneath the waters—deep beneath the fire . . . lies a place of exquisite light and healing.' I had conquered the fire on another journey and had no real fear of this pit now; even if I had I should at this moment have welcomed the thought of total consumption and destruction. I looked round for the child, who was so transformed now that it was obvious he needed neither feeding nor carrying; he could walk quite easily, hand in hand with me. Gently I explained to him what we were going to do, that there was no need to be afraid, and that I thought we were almost at the end of our journey. He now trusted me completely, and hand in hand, followed by Gildas, we plunged into the pit of flames. I was not aware of any pain or of being consumed as we plunged downwards to the centre of the fire, indeed the flames seemed hardly to touch us and my only sensation was one of being cleansed, purified, re-made, so that I no longer wanted to cast off my body as being evil and filthy. I opened myself to the cleansing powers of the fire and was filled again with the will to go onwards and complete my task, not only in this journey but in the one to follow also.

At the centre of the fire a kind of archway led on to a dark passage and along this passage we journeyed for some time, the child and I, hand in hand, Gildas following behind. At last we saw the light at the end of the tunnel and though footsore and weary we quickened our pace and journeyed towards it, but as we approached the source of light we slowed down, and had I been wearing shoes I should have removed them, so strong was the sensation that here was holy ground. We came to a part of the tunnel where there was a break in the roof, and light of a beautiful healing quality flowed down upon us. Now before us was a simple wooden door and at the door a guardian with a golden staff. Standing before the door he addressed us : 'Whence come you and what is your mission?' And I answering said, 'We come from a place of light and have journeyed through darkness and tribulation to bring to this place of healing and regeneration this soul whom in a past life I have led astray and cast into the mire; and, by our journey here, I have been told that some of this heavy karma shall be redeemed.'

Then the guardian flung open the door and said, 'Then you are welcome to enter the outer sanctuary. This child must now go on ahead of you, but you may be assured that he will be healed and strengthened and all will be well.'

We came now into a place full of light, ever changing in colour, but not in beauty and quality. The chamber was circular, and when we came to its centre where a jewelled hexagon within a circle was engraved upon the floor, I knelt in peace as the guardian took the child to some further place. Peace and beauty enfolded and healed me; all my heaviness was dispelled and soon, with Gildas, I floated upwards away from this place and away from the regions of darkness above, to that lovely familiar world where at last my Guide's lips were unsealed and his arms opened to receive me in a loving embrace.

CHAPTER 12

The Sixth Journey

May to July 1964

This journey differed from all the others. In June, in a letter to Mary, I wrote:

'It is quite different in the way I am experiencing it; there is no conflict or tension between the two worlds, and because of this none of the mental exhaustion and despair which have really been the main trial before. It is difficult to put into words how I feel, but the inner and the outer no longer impinge the one upon the other, and I can live normally and cheerfully on the mundane level *without that anguishing and supreme effort* which has been required before, when the waters of the inner journey close over me. I suffer and am conscious of the darkness of my journey and each incident is as vivid as ever, yet at last I can let it happen and absorb the lessons of the imagery without continually fighting and being afraid, and thus through tension increasing my pain. I shall die a death of some finality and at last be *painlessly* re-born.'

* * * * *

On Whit Monday, May 18th, with Gildas beside me, I stood on the brink of a deep dark pool and knew the Sixth Journey was about to begin. Together we plunged into the waters and were taken in the suction of a whirlpool to be dragged into the depths. As we descended, we came into that deep blackness which is blacker than black; the atmosphere was oppressive in the extreme, yet still the descent continued. (This descent in complete darkness and oppression lasted for just over a fortnight.)

Suddenly the extreme darkness was penetrated by a great and intense white light, and the whirlpool ceased as we fell at a great rate down a narrow shaft to the centre of a great white-hot fire. The heat was uncomfortable in the extreme, yet we were not consumed. At the centre of the fire was a coal which glowed exceedingly brightly and gave off a great heat. I knew that I must pluck this coal from the fire. I tried many times but the heat was such that I could not bear the pain of grasping this coal. At last with a supreme effort I grasped and held it, and though it felt as though my flesh was seared and even the bones of my hand charred, I did not relinquish my hold. Just when I could bear it no longer, the pain of burning ceased; my hand was uninjured and in the palm lay a perfect sphere of pure gold. Gildas produced a chain; the sphere by some process was welded to it and then it was fastened about my wrist.

Later, we were in a tunnel, buffeted and carried by a great wind. Sometimes we were blown forward at a great pace, at others we could not progress for the wind would blow us back. At all times we were cast against jagged edges of rock, our bodies bruised and bleeding, and our clothes torn. Once more it was very dark.

After quite a long time we seemed to come to the end of the tunnel, or rather, a dead end; it was dark but as far as I could tell we were confronted with a great mass of soft soil. The wind was less now, but seemed to be blowing us ever onwards, and Gildas, by a sign, made me know that it was right to go on and not back. Yet now a sudden terror and panic gripped me. I could not—would not—go on, burrowing my way like some animal through the soft moist earth; the time had come which I dreaded would come upon each journey: *I could not go on*. The horror of going forward which gripped me I knew I should never overcome alone; there could be no going back, and so in this place I should die and fail and all my previous sufferings would be to no end and no avail. I think this was the blackest moment of all the journeys, and, through the days that followed, the *only* time when this last journey had repercussions in the outer world, making me heavy and miserable, utterly wretched at all levels.

As I curled myself into a ball trying to shut out everything around me, Gildas gave me a gentle look of compassion and himself began to dig at the mass of soft earth. All my love for him rose within me, yet not even that was enough to make me rise and go forward together with my Guide. I had no will to ask for help or light; I craved death; all my will to emerge triumphant from this last journey ebbed away, and I sat alone and suffering in the darkness. Soon I realized that the warm moist earth was all around me and I was entombed in the mass through which I was so afraid to pass. Strangely, although I still could not go on, the warmth and moisture of the earth gave me a feeling of security, and a sense of tranquillity mingled uneasily with my fears and despair. At last I slept within the womb of the earth, and in my slumber my conflict died and a great and wonderful regeneration took place within me. As in a dream, I relived some of the terrors of previous journeys, but always I had come through, and the struggle had always been easier when I had been able to submit myself with faith and trust to that greater Spirit which can bring us unerringly through all things. When I awoke, the last vestige of my panic, dread and rebellion seemed to be wiped from me, and I reached a total acceptance of all that should be required or asked of me in this life. Now I relaxed within this warm, moist earth womb, and felt the texture about me with a sensuous delight, and knew that at last I was ready for a final rebirth; that the pain was past, the burden shed, and joy was to come.

Relaxed and at peace at last I now felt the urge to go on through the dark earth to the light. There was no fear now, nor horror of 'burrowing like an animal'. I could go easily forward, and I enjoyed the sensation of moving through the warm, moist earth. I moved in a rhythm, pushing forward and then relaxing, then on again. I did not hurry or fight against anything; I was content to go at an easy pace, using my strength carefully, not wishing for all to be over and fretting to reach the light, nor yet wanting to go back. I was not afraid to go on, but I lived each moment to the full and was aware only of the present. After some time a tinge of excitement touched me and I knew I was coming ever nearer to the light. Now my rhythm did change; I pushed my way forward with more effort and determination and my periods of relaxation became less and less; then at last with a final great effort I pushed through the last great wall of earth and, with Gildas beside me, emerged, new-born, into the light. At first the brightness was dazzling and the atmosphere seemed chill after the warm earth. I was exhausted, although I had not noticed it before, and there was a moment of insecurity as I left the earth behind; but this was a brief moment and then something warm was wrapped around me, strong arms gently carried me, then with the love of Gildas encircling me, secure and warm, I slept in complete peace, and on waking was refreshed, light-hearted, and full of joy.

Gildas led me to a gentle stream where I bathed and put on a pure white robe, then together we went to a peaceful place, a kind of glade surrounded by trees, and Gildas bade me sit upon some soft green moss and meditate. I sat and closed my eyes and drank in the peace of this spot, but was not really deep in meditation. Then I opened my eyes and was amazed to find that the quiet green glade had receded, and I sat at the centre of a great hexagonal temple of light. Each section of the hexagon was made up of a different coloured light, as I had seen it before : red, green, blue, yellow, white and purple, and the centre was flooded with light of gold and silver; the beauty and the atmosphere were indescribable. In each section of the hexagon stood a 'being' apparelled in the same colour as the light in that section. Led by Gildas I knelt before each one of these, and received from each a kiss upon the crown of my head. Finally I returned to the centre of the temple of light, and the blaze of gold and silver light became intense, until, looking down, I saw that my robe was no longer white but glowed gold and silver as though made from the light itself, and in my hands I had the golden orb, plucked from the very centre of the fire near the beginning of the journey. It was as if I were no longer a separate entity; Gildas, the 'beings', the temple, and myself were caught up, light as air, as one with the very light which went to make up this wondrous temple; time ceased to exist, so that the ecstasy could have lasted a thousand years or for a fleeting second. Yet at last all things were understood, the suffering and the joy, the labour and the peace were one, bound about with light and beyond the light with darkness; for here all things had their place and the very harmony of feeling became music in my ears, rising to a crescendo, then gradually fading, until I stood, alone, with Gildas, and the final journey was over and all was well.

CHAPTER 13

Psychological Experience and the Ageless Wisdom

By Mary

September 1964

The intensive work of the past seven years had been almost entirely on psychological, emotional and intuitional levels, the insights being in feeling rather than in concepts.

The Sixth Journey finished in July. In August Gildas recommended that we gain some perspective by intellectual consolidation in a wider context. He suggested that we should study the journeys 'in every aspect as a whole, and extract from them the finer degrees of meaning and teaching'. Especially he asked us to 'begin to understand something of the progressive spiritual revelation behind them'. This we attempted to do during the next few years.

To start the ball rolling, while on a somewhat strenuous fortnight's holiday in September on the Dorset coast (the only chance I had), I wrote three commentaries: Freudian, Jungian, and this one. (Later a friend kindly supplied a fourth: an Astrological commentary.) These three were written entirely 'off the cuff' with no reference books at hand, being sent to Ruth as private letters—essays to act as a basis for our future discussions. The psychological aspects have already been dealt with in Chapter One of this book. Presenting the spiritual commentary here, in its appropriate time-context, I am well aware of its inadequacy, but—in the interests of keeping a true record—I reproduce it exactly as it was written at the time, and I trust that readers will take it in this spirit.

Ten years later, however, were I writing it now, I think that the chief alteration I would make would be an idiomatic one: instead of using the image of 'subtle bodies' I would adopt the term 'energy fields', and would refer to all the recent research on the subject.

* * * * *

In esoteric teaching, the 'spheres' or 'planes' of other-world experience are believed to be as real as is our earth experience, if not more so—more so in so far as they are formed of 'matter' vibrating at higher frequencies so that everything appears to be more intensely alive. These planes of varying frequencies interpenetrate one another, including our dense material earth, in much the same way as air, salt and water interpenetrate a sponge, or—a better image—as radio waves of various length co-exist without interference.

Different schools give their own terms to these degrees but, generally speaking, they are:

The Etheric Plane   (next to the earth, the vital replica).
The Astral Plane   (plane of finer substance, responsive to feeling and emotion).
The Mental Plane   (plane of the higher mind, of thought and form).
The Celestial Plane   (perceived mainly by intuition, formless light, largely beyond description).
. . . and so on, beyond our ken.

In the East, it has been recognized for a long time that man has subtle bodies, apart from the physical body. Some schools recognize seven bodies altogether, each of which corresponds to, and functions in, a plane of its own reality. Just as these planes interpenetrate, so do our bodies. According to the level of our consciousness, so we are aware of the corresponding rate of vibration manifesting in apparently solid form in what appears to be a 'real' environment around us. For we have senses at every level, and in esoteric schools we are taught that one of the purposes of meditation is to develop these higher senses so that the more subtle worlds will gradually become available to us. Most people are too much locked in their physical bodies to do this, but a few are able to become aware at least on the Astral plane.

The Etheric Body is so closely attached to the physical body that —The coarser part of it 'dies' very soon after physical death.

The Astral Body functions in the Astral world—the 'heaven' or 'hell' of tradition. The subtle material of the Astral plane surrounds us and is malleable by our feelings and attitudes so that all the time we are building our own heavens and hells and intermediary states to which, quite automatically, we are drawn on casting off the physical sheath, whether in sleep or in death. At its highest, this is the realm of light and extreme beauty, with radiant flowers and wonderful colour and sound—the 'Summerland' of the spiritualists. Many of the intermediate states (Purgatory?) have conditions very similar to the earth. At its lowest are the hells of the Lower Astral with terrifying appearances, darkness, and pain. There are many books descriptive of journeys into the dark Astral by people who do rescue work there; all speak of the gloom, heaviness, barren landscape, cold, and slow vibrations. I am describing the apparent nature of the Astral *environment*, although I realize I am supposed to be writing of the Astral *body*; but this is in order, because according to the body we have built is the environment perceived. Further, whether 'higher' or 'lower', undimmed by the flesh covering, emotions are extremely acute in the Astral realm, both painful and pleasurable.

The Mental Body is the body of thought which functions in the mental plane of pattern and design. In meditation, this realm is often perceived in the form of the geometric symbolism of cross, star, triangle, etc. Being beyond the Astral, one functions here beyond emotion, but these forms are immensely creative.

The Celestial Body—termed by some schools the Ego (not to be confused with the Freudian ego)—works on the principle of intuition; in meditation it can be reached in the 'timeless moments' when time as we know it is transcended. At this—and higher—levels, we experience that sense of union with all things which is known as cosmic consciousness.

Application of the Theory to the Journeys

I would suggest that in your journeys you have functioned throughout the range of these bodies and their corresponding planes, from the depths to the heights. As I see it, you worked mostly on the Astral, both higher and lower (and intermediate), but a good many visions, symbols and teachings were characteristic of the Mental plane. The greater moments of awareness (e.g. on the Pennines above Darwen and during the initiations, and especially the final experience of the Sixth Journey) would correspond to the fourth level.

The bulk of the work, however, seems to have been done on the Astral level. Because the Astral is a world created largely by our own emotional attitudes, others do not necessarily see it as we do; thus on your Third Journey Gildas and Michael, although with you on the journey, did not experience the conditions as darkly as you did.

The journeys proper were all visits to what is called the 'Lower Astral' or the 'Hells' (see Swedenborg's writings and Dante's *Inferno*), in order to redeem and transmute the dark karma of yourself and humanity, raising the frequency of the vibrations, making the dark conditions lighter, the cold conditions warmer.

In between the journeys proper, during the interludes, you appear to have worked on the intermediate Astral planes which are not so very different from earth, yet where work still has to be done, e.g. working with the children, re-building the house, etc. These realms do not have the terrible heaviness, darkness and coldness of the hells. These intermediate planes, I suggest, would correspond to Dante's *Purgatorio* which is by no means necessarily unpleasant but is *a place of learning*. Then at times of peace and achievement, and the long, quiet periods with Gildas when life is tranquil and wonderful, I should say that you rise to the true home of your spirit in one of the 'heavens' of the higher Astral planes where all is light and love and beauty. At certain special times, e.g. when preparing to undertake a journey, or during an initiation, you are most certainly called to still higher levels which appear in some ways to resemble the *Paradiso* of Dante.

At the start of a journey you nearly always report a sensation of diving, climbing or sinking down, or of being drawn down through a whirlpool or vortex. In this process, the vibrational frequency of your bodies is being progressively reduced, so that you automatically sink and become slow, inert and cold even on the hottest summer day. (In some mythologies hell is cold.) The slower the vibrationary rate, the more dense and resistant is the environmental 'material' with which you have to deal (slime, mud, rock etc.) I think this may be why Gildas suggested a light, meatless diet with sun-ripened fruits during one of the worst journeys, because this would not weigh you down still further as would meat.

Conversely, when you 'float up' after a journey, having shed your load—or rather transformed it—your vibrations are raised in frequency so that automatically you soar to the equivalent level. The whole process resembles the transformations of water, doesn't it? Water-vapour to water, then to solid ice, then back to water and to water-vapour again; all quite scientific but the changes appear to be at a more basic atomic than a molecular level.

In the dark and heavy spheres, the lower frequencies have to be transformed by you, as agent, using light and love as transforming power. In this way, the landscapes, animals, and appearances generally change their nature. When I say 'appearances', I do not mean, of course, that these are purely subjective in the sense of illusions or hallucinations; I mean that the basic energy of the cosmos can manifest as dense or as radiant substance according to the speed of vibration of the particles composing it. Hence (as I understand him) Gildas' saying that the light is always the healing and redemptive power. Light quickens, transmutes, just as does the heat of the 'fire' in alchemy, transforming base metals into gold. Ordinary cooking has the same symbolism. Basically, all this is extremely simple. Apply heat—light—love, and the dense thing or person begins to warm up and glow and become lighter—but oh how difficult sometimes in practice! Thus, often in your journeys the mantra of the Lord's Prayer, or any prayer for—or symbol of—the light, has done the trick, transforming the dark and heavy appearances.

This is the 'Great Work' of which the alchemists write, the redemptive vocation symbolised, I would suggest, by your former urge to do missionary work in 'Darkest Africa' (the 'dark continent', standing symbolically for the primitive, possibly decadent aspect of our own libido, yet at the same time the raw potential, the untapped strength in us all). In much the same way, the black magic and voodoo of Africa is now being painfully transformed through African humanity as the new nations arise and 'civilize' themselves to bring in new life to the planet. Some souls —a good many I should guess at the present time—have volunteered on the inner planes to do such work, each helping in his individual way as the whole planet, together with its envelopes of subtler spheres, moves (very rapidly now) up into the light, the frequency rate changing just about as fast as human kind can bear it.

According to esoteric teaching, we are very close to a period of planetary initiation. We are the instruments, and the present emphasis, before the 'changes' occur, is on healing as many people as possible so that they can benefit. As you know, spiritual healing works mainly by light, quickening the rate of vibration in the body of the sufferer, so that his increased life-force throws off the dark slow elements due to disease. A diseased organ manifests to clairvoyant sight as a dark patch in the aura, disease being the reverse of 'quickening'.

Thus, all the great soul-journeys are journeys into change of condition—change of the wave-length to which we 'tune in'.

Subjective and Objective 'Worlds': Man as a Creative Instrument

We can now begin to understand and resolve the apparent distinction between the 'objective' and 'subjective' existence of the inner world—a seeming contradiction which is reconcilable only at a higher level of awareness. To the extent that we (our feelings and attitudes) *are* our Astral surround, the inner heavens, hells, and intermediate conditions are subjective. (This works even to some extent on earth where people go around shrouded in gloom, always seeing life as hostile, or, on the other hand, attract joy to themselves by their positive outlook.) In one sense, then, all our experience on the Astral planes is a 'magic shadow show' of illusion—illusion in so far as it is the product of our own projected feelings. Only to the extent to which we are compulsively attached to certain beliefs do they become 'real' for us, affecting us painfully or otherwise. Thus, before you passed through your fire initiation, your beliefs about the destructive power of fire caused extreme pain and fear, but, once through, you could use the fire at will for purification without fear, pain, or destructiveness. What had changed was your 'feeling-concept' about the nature of fire.

Yet, if we *are* attached, these appearances seem real enough! If 'thought are things', then the subtle Astral substance and the still more rarefied Mental patterns are modified by our feelings and thoughts so that we do actually create a world. *Man is essentially a creative instrument* with power to build, destroy, transmute. He does this by attitude and imagination. Hence the importance in education of training attitudes and imagination. It is a fearsome thought, the power we have! As I understand it, it is in this sense that 'Ye are Gods'—gods in embryo—learning through pain and suffering and joy, and through the hurting and healing of others by what we create, to exercise our creative function. This creative principle works, of course, in our material world too, but, having to 'crystallize out' by means of physical and mechanical labour in solid three-dimensional matter, it takes longer. Yet it is instructive to remember that everything man has made on this planet was at first a thought and a feeling—a blue-print in the Mental and Astral. Slums, Coventry Cathedral —all of it.

In this way, spiritual healing, so-called 'faith-healing', Radionics, Radiesthesia, and other forms of 'fringe medicine' work on the more subtle bodies, the effects later following through into the physical. Even within a special branch such as Radionics, for example, which has probably worked primarily on the Etheric level, some practitioners nowadays are dispensing with blood-spots and are concentrating more on broadcasting positive thought and feeling—very close to spiritual healing.

Different healers work on different levels—Magnetic, Etheric, Spiritual. Psychologists, I suppose, are concerned mainly with the Astral work.

Here lies a big responsibility; in the higher levels of healing we find that we must not try to do the work with our lower minds, willing what we consider from the small ego ought to happen. Indeed, the less the intellect *interferes* the better, though it is useful when it takes its rightful place in co-operating with the trained faculty of intuition. The work is done from the higher self. Thus, in spiritual healing we are taught simply to hold the person who is sick or troubled *in the light* by the use of controlled creative imagination, but without introducing any personal feelings, hopes, fears, power-ideas or wants at all—simply handing them over to God. What we contribute is the vibration of light as far as we can imagine it; those on the other side then add their power to amplify our contribution. We are told that the quality of the human essence, at the lower rate of vibration, is a necessary ingredient without which it is difficult for them to reach and heal another person still in the flesh. We contribute the lower current, as it were.

Again, light is a specific against apparently objective appearances. Thus, a person whose consciousness is vibrating at a low frequency *sees* his environment in the inner world in the forms characteristic of that frequency. People with Delirium Tremens have lowered their vibrations to the point where they actually do see some of the denizens of the Lower Astral! It is on this level that we can understand some of the apparitions which the Knights of the Round Table met in the primaeval forests, and can see why the Cross of Light was proof against them. (I have told an untrained psychic, who was too open, to use the cross within the circle of light and she had no more trouble.) In dreams, the light will dissolve a monster, and the great thing to remember in all this inner work is that light is positive, darkness negative. You can take a light into a dark room and it becomes light, but you cannot take a dark into a light room to make it dark. The light, by its very nature, will *always* conquer the darkness.

A person whose consciousness is vibrating at a higher

frequency perceives corresponding forms in the Astral—exquisite landscapes, trees and flowers scintillating with life and light, sparkling energizing water and so on. So, something which has always interested me as a former geographer : because of our own selectivity, our environment is not purely an objective phenomenon even on this earth-plane; just as we pick out a particular wave-length on the radio so, largely unconsciously, we select what we perceive.

This explains not only the landscapes but also the people with whom we associate in the various spheres. People in the intermediate spheres appear much as on earth; in higher spheres they are progressively more beautiful with illumined faces, radiant robes, and with their large auras of many colours shining around them. In the lower spheres are those who have let themselves go right down to the worse-than-bestial level and are ugly, misshapen, stinking creatures at their worst. Here is the 'mission field'—the darkest Africa—and bands of people from the higher spheres 'cloak themselves', as they term it, in darker raiment so that their light does not shock and blind the inhabitants. We are told that they cannot remain for too long at a time without returning for healing and refeshment themselves to the higher levels. Here on earth we all mix up; we cannot get away from others of a different kind even if we would, for it is through this mixing that we learn our lessons. But when we shed the physical body, then the law of 'gravitation', or of 'finding one's own level' according to degree of light, works completely automatically, so that each person goes to his own place along with others of his own kind. If he were to go higher, except for brief visits, he could not stand the conditions, so this is a merciful provision.

According to spiritualist, theosophical, and ancient-wisdom teaching, these beings are not merely 'ego split-offs' nor even archetypal personifications fragmented from the total Self; they are persons existing in their own right. Functioning in the fuller life, they are far more fully alive and far-seeing than are we in our 'little boxes' of three dimensions who see 'through a glass darkly'. In our higher selves we know them, and know ourselves as we are known. It is indeed a relief that they know us better than we can know ourselves, down here, so that to the extent to which we have surrendered the separateness of the little ego, by them we can be used, lived through, 'controlled' (in a positive sense with our full co-operation—never obsessed). Their lives— the life of God stepped down through the 'resistances' of many beings at different levels, as though through a series of trans- formers—is lived eventually in us, not our own ego-life alone. This, I suggest, is what is meant by 'You do not work in your own strength'. Yet we always have free will, and the higher beings will never interfere with this. They and we are instru- ments of God operating each at our own level.

Whilst, however, higher beings will always inspire and use us wisely if we open ourselves to God, we must be very careful in this work never to open ourselves to the lower beings who will latch themselves on to any weakness in our personalities, and, having no regard for free will, will certainly obsess us if they can. It is believed that a good deal of obsessional neurosis and certain psychoses can be due to obsession by other entities rather than by one's own fixed ideas, although of course it is one's own attitude which attracts the entities in the first place. Thus, be- fore undertaking development, it is of the utmost importance that we should have worked on our personalities to make them strong, healthy and balanced. In such work, we first clear out our own Augean stables (the dark side of the individual unconscious) and then, as Jung would agree, we can continue to work on a small piece of the collective unconscious of humanity as a whole. This, I would imagine, is what Gildas meant when he said to you that in these journeys you help others and the world more than you realise (through direct *inward* action?) When we reach the collective level, as Jungians know, there is a 'Geography' of the inner world which, though differing in detail for each indi- vidual, is common to all in its basic landmarks. In all the great myths and hero-journeys, in all the descriptions of the 'planes' and 'spheres' by spiritual guides, there are basic similarities. At the outset comes the 'Call'; very soon afterwards one meets one's guide. Each soul has a personal guide as well as a guardian angel and also (when on the path) various teachers who may change from time to time as the need arises. And later, at a certain stage on the path, when one has committed oneself as a dedicated instrument in however humble a capacity as a neophyte, one is attached to a Master (especially when following a teacher (guru) or an esoteric group or school). The Master is rarely contacted; mainly on special occasions (e.g. your initiation) and always at higher levels.

Communication between Different Levels and the Function of the Symbol

Physicists are beginning to get very close to the ancient wisdom teaching about the nature of matter, seeing it in terms of primal energy, cosmic creative power, very like 'Divine Mind' as one said. As we go higher in the planes of consciousness, so the cosmic energy manifests more directly and powerfully, less stepped down, less modified by resistance into form. Thus, in meditation we start from the dense, hard, resistant world we know which may be likened to the hard 'finger nail' of the cosmic organism, scratching the outer crust of things; we then penetrate up through the changing, malleable colours and substance of the Astral, the patterns and designs of the Mental, and beyond we find there is a world of formlessness which may at first be frightening— pure light, pure energy—intensely alive and powerful, but nothing to which our senses can attach themselves except perhaps through the highest awareness of love. Dante describes this in the *Paradiso*.

Mankind needs a *language*—a form of communication—between the ineffable all-ness of the formless levels of cosmic consciousness right down through to the pastry burning in the oven! As I see it, the language which is most meaningful at every level is the *symbol*. Throughout history, universal truths have been enshrined in symbols which everyone can understand, each in his own way, at every grade of significance. Thus, a figure of 'Our Lady' may be a very 'down-here' object to the church worker who cleans her up regularly and notes that the paint is coming off! To others in vision she mediates the Divine Mother —she is a channel. To yet others, she *is* the Divine Mother. Again, anyone looking up a symbol in a dictionary of symbolism will at first be confused by the many different meanings and values—often quite opposite—attached to the same symbol. We who work in the world of psychotherapy, using dreams and paintings, know that from the one symbol (e.g. snake) the individual selects the meaning which is significant for him at a certain period of growth; later the same symbol may well have taken over another significance.

For symbols, unlike signs (which are just something standing for something else), are always alive, capable of change and growth, pregnant with creative meaning, evocative; they have the power to mediate experience, often of great intensity, to transform the divine impact of the numinous into a kind of confrontation which can be apprehended by the human. The symbol, as Jung has shown, actually acts as transformer. Hence in your journeys the use of the phrase: 'The transforming symbol.'

On the Astral level, we may well use them merely as signs; Gildas, for instance, puts on a black robe at the outset of a journey. This may be a sign of what is going to happen; or it may well be the 'cloak' as I have described earlier with which he has to cover his light when descending to the dark spheres. But your real symbols had immense power in themselves to transform and were meaningful at many levels; we spent a long time trying to understand them in relation to the outer world. Such were the octopus, the tentacle of which became the golden rod; the golden flower; and, of course, the jewel, symbol of the Deep Centre—the Self—the Treasure. (Compare the diamond body of the Eastern mystics.) These are all channels for concentrated light and power, and (as we see if we study the Egyptian mysteries) concentrated patterns of light, using a symbol to carry the light, will always conquer astral images of elementals. Take Gildas' sword as an example, or the protective power of the cross within the circle of light. Direct light, of course, would do it, but mankind finds it very difficult, living in a world of form and substance, to focus formless light direct, hence the use of the properties of the Mental and Astral planes to give form and substance in the shape of a symbol which can carry the quality of consciousness needed (e.g. the quality of wholeness in the six-pointed star).

Symbols, and the myths which contain them, are the language linking higher and lower frequencies, inner and outer worlds, subjective and objective appearances, the abstract and the concrete. This is why they often appear paradoxical, because they unite apparent opposites. So this leads on to a study of symbols in your inner world in detail, which, I hope, will follow one day.

CHAPTER 14

Preparation for the Seventh Journey

(Mainly) January to June 1968

By Mary

In August 1965, I had taken a piece of Ruth's hair (as a link) to a very reliable sensitive. This woman 'saw' Ruth as a 'child of light'. She felt that Ruth had been through almost every form of experience on the *inner*, between lives, but that the present life was the first of a new set of experiences in which the two aspects would meet together as one; she spoke of 'a first incarnation on a higher rung of the ladder of *earthly* incarnation'. When I told her (afterwards) about Gildas, she said she would be grateful if he would check and comment on her own findings. (This explanation is necessary to give the background of Gildas' reply):

'These things are so difficult to explain without going into great detail about cosmology, and this I am not yet prepared to do; it is not the right time. There is much practical learning and living to be done first, but later the time will come when you *shall* ask all these questions which fascinate you so, and be given full and careful answers. With the coming of the Age of Gold you will know all these things anyway through direct vision and awareness, so be patient, my dears, let all unfold as it has been ordered, and trust in the promises you have been given.

'I will, however, without too much detail, try to make things clearer for you. The general impression gained by anyone "tuning in" to your vibration *would* be that you are "a child of

189

light", for you have incarnated in the far past into very sheltered conditions. You have trodden the way of the neophyte in the temples of truth and light of the ancient wisdom, and on through the ages you have lived on earth the pure life of the "religieuse" and the mystic. You incarnated into times of peace and plenty and right values, and it was easy for you to tread the path of Light. For long ages you knew little of evil; you were pure and innocent. Yet purity and innocence are not enough; the evolved soul must experience every side of life—must know each facet of the jewel. Not all the lessons learned by a soul are learned in incarnation. From our planes, souls are given the opportunity to experience with, and to influence for good or evil, the lives of those who move within the limitations of the body, and through this experience and influencing so the evolution of the soul continues on either side of the "veil".

'From these planes you determined to learn of the darker side of life, and soon that which previously you had ignored became your fascination. You led many astray, you allowed your spirit to be used to convince others that the path of evil held more power and reward than the path of light. You entered into the "vacant" bodies of "dark mediums" to give forth messages of power and conviction. You influenced innocent virgins so that they took part in base rites and orgies. You did not misuse your own body, but you delighted in that misuse which others made of theirs.

'Do not be distressed, my child; these things *are* and have to be. Remember that at the greatest heights and the utmost depths all things are finally one. You grew strong in evil, and, though it has to be redeemed, when once you turned finally to the light, you brought with you this strength to use in the positive spheres of life, and the soul which now incarnates does so indeed on a "higher rung of the ladder". Having learned something of the highest, lightest, most free and innocent side of life, and having also the knowledge of evil, you tread now the higher paths where integration is learned and past experience put to more positive use. With your recent, total dedication of the "ego", you are indeed on the right "wavelength"; the way lies before you, and all in its own time shall be revealed and fulfilled.'

*　　*　　*　　*　　*

In view of the significance of the hexagon and the number six, we had assumed that the series of journeys had ended with the sixth, in July 1964. Three and a half years later, however, in January 1968—and just at the most critical period of sending out Gildas' teaching after the crisis of Christmas 1967 (see *Gildas Communicates*)—I received a letter from Ruth. She told me that Gildas had suddenly gone away, without explanation, and that she was suffering both physically and mentally. She had no idea when he would return, nor of the reason for his going.

This was a shock, especially in view of all that he had asked us to do. But we could only accept and work on whatever came —and these were dreams.

Ruth found herself bothered by four compulsive and recurrent dreams. I encouraged her to write them, together with her associations, which she did :

'In the first dream I am being shown round a large new building—perhaps a school? I am unhappy, restless and highly critical of all I am shown. For a *new* building there seems to be an awful lot of very old-fashioned ideas incorporated—high windows and classrooms leading off a hall. The whole is unsatisfactory and incongruous. Then we come to a door which keeps opening and shutting all the time on its own. As soon as it closes it will swing open again and then close immediately, only to open once more. My guide professes puzzlement at the workings of such a door. In a flash of insight, since no workings are visible, I say it is obviously done by an electro-magnetic device, the current being constantly broken and completed by the movement of the door.

'In the second dream I am holding a Japanese fan; it is elaborately decorated with black and gold on a white background. The main motif running the full width of the fan is a black dragon with golden spines, and golden nostrils giving forth black smoke which forms into the strange symbols that are the borders of the fan. I have a strange feeling that if I could understand the symbols, I should achieve peace of mind and serenity, but they remain only symbols no matter how hard I try to extract meaning from them.

'In the third dream I am going up a steep rocky staircase. It is rather perilous with sharp dips all round, and I go up until I can no longer see the ground. Now each step becomes higher and higher; I decide that I can go no further so will return to the bottom, but when I look round I see that the steps below me have disappeared; there is nothing, only a sheer cliff face. I cannot go down, I cannot make the effort to go on. Precariously perched, I am terrified, then everything turns to ice and I wake up shivering and panic-stricken.

'In the fourth dream I am black with a white "shadow" which does all that I do, like an ordinary shadow cast by the sun, but yet which is also separate from me. I stand, naked and black, before a pool of slimy dirty water; my shadow stands on the opposite side of the pool—we are facing—and suddenly we both dive in. (I think "I" am feminine and my shadow is masculine.) I lie inert and uncaring in the deep mud at the bottom of the pool, and my shadow does likewise. A long time passes, then the mud begins to move and contract, propelling me forward, like a womb. Suddenly, my shadow comes and lies on top of me and is absorbed into me, and I accept this without any feeling at all; I am very passive, letting things happen to me, not fighting back. The contractions continue and suddenly I am expelled forcefully from the mud and born into a world of fire. Now I realize that the shadow had foreknowledge and went within for protection, but apart from this realization, and a little anger which comes with it, I remain passive in the midst of the fire. It sears my skin, but it is as though from within I am unconnected with my body, and I do not attempt to escape or to fight the pain; only the shadow cringes within, but I remain unmoved until the fire burns itself out leaving me scorched and suffering a pain I refuse to recognize, but in one piece. I bury myself in the ashes of the fire and remain still for a long time. I feel vaguely ruffled and annoyed when a great wind springs up and blows away the ashes, and rouse myself sufficiently to know that my pain has been healed and my black skin made whole once more. The wind increases, I am blown against rocks, blinded by sand in a desert, tossed by ruthless waves in a stormy sea. I remain silent, unfeeling, not caring whether I live or die, but the shadow within craves life and protects itself at all times against the dangers that beset us and the pains which are inflicted upon me. (I wake up with a feeling of unease and incompletion, as though this dream is not yet ended, but each time I have dreamed it, it has ended at the same point.)'

* * * * *

In order to try to work on these dreams, we managed to meet for one night in February in a hotel, near Ruth's home. The following detailed account shows the amount that can be done in a short but intensive period of our time when regular sessions are impracticable. It may also serve to give readers a picture of the process linking personal dream-work with that of the deeper journeys.

In the early evening Ruth 'went into' three of the dreams in turn, allowing the images to develop. I wrote down what she said, *verbatim*.

'The first dream has an added bit: in the hall is a bird-cage in which is an egg. The egg hatches into a black eagle, but as soon as the bird beats with its wings against the top of the cage, it turns back into an egg again.

'The second dream: the black smoke needs understanding *for itself*, not transmuting.

'The fourth dream: in some ways all this is a terrific test of faith. I was supposed to be preparing for another initiation ... I sometimes feel I've been in the clouds for years. There's only one reality: *life as it is*. The "white self" is not real. I wish I were even sure of experience with Gildas; what I'm tempted to do is to give it all up and live in the here-and-now.'

I accepted this as valid and useful doubt, and we discussed criticisms which had been made of the teachings, and the need for balance and discrimination and for challenging everything. What had we that we *could* be sure of? Only that the writings were there and that people recognize their quality. This is an indisputable *fact*. How do they come? Not from Ruth herself, as she is. Later in the evening we did more work on the fourth dream. Ruth went right into it, and reported:

'Right down in the centre of the earth is a black sea. The black self wants to dive in (and get it over) but could not sufficiently protect the white self if it did. Alone, the black self is nothing but a shell; it would disintegrate without the white one within. The white one is too weak; they need to fuse—to integrate. The white needs some of the strength of the black.'

I questioned why they could not carry on as before, the black shell protecting the white self.

'Because the white self is too big.'

During the night, the first dream was continued. The black eagle did not turn back to an egg, but to a miniature white eagle, perfectly formed, not a chick. When it tried to fly, however, it had to become a black eagle again.

The following morning, over early tea, we worked on the third dream, so far untouched. Ruth went into the dream, with long periods of silence :

'There's an awful feeling of panic . . . I can't stay there, not for long, I'd fall off.'

I suggested that we both invoked all the help we could, from higher sources.

'The panic is getting worse . . . whilst the ice is there I can't fall. I have to wait for the ice to melt. Ice? There's a rigid control I try to exercise—that's the ice. I can't move yet; I'm frozen to the rock . . . I *have* to let the ice melt.'

I suggested a phantasy of what would happen if it melted, so that we could try to understand the nature of the panic.

'I might get washed down . . . everything would turn to mud . . . I'd be floundering in the mud. The rock would turn soft . . . the panic is horrible—but the ice is clean and safe and clear to a certain extent.'

We discussed ice and hard rock in terms of defences. What would the mud be?

'I don't know . . . I can't trust myself to it . . . it's too sticky and dirty . . .' (Long pause.)

'Nothing happening?'

'Yes, in a way . . . a sort of going between the opposites, the ice and the mud. I can't concentrate on either of them . . . it's a bit like the door (in the first dream) keeping on changing. One is clear and clean, the other so dirty and sticky . . .' (Long pause while continuously shooting between one and the other.)

'Oh, I'm so terrified, the ice is melting, not just in phantasy, but really. The whole cliff is turning into a sea of mud! I'm in the mud. The ice isn't there to get back to . . . If I stay at the bottom of the mud I shall suffocate.'

Although I had invoked all the spiritual help I could, I had previously been quite detached from Ruth's experience, but at this point I found myself seeing and knowing it, though not actually being in it. I just saw and knew that the mud was rapidly thinning to water, and that Ruth was rising through it, swimming up, breaking the surface, into the light. This was incredibly rapid—a few seconds—whereas the previous part had taken a long time. The process seemed to transcend time. Ruth said :

'I feel better. I can swim. The sun is shining . . . Like a swan on a black sea . . . the swan has a golden body . . . its wings are black underneath and white on the top. The black absorbs strength from the black sea; the white reflects the sunlight.'

(At this stage in the transformation we stopped for bath and breakfast!)

After breakfast, we worked on the second dream, the most difficult to understand.

'I can't get *into* him (the dragon). He just breathes, in and out . . . He's trying to *communicate* with smoke . . . he's blind . . . I don't know how to get in, he's so hard and scaly.'

I commented that traditionally every dragon has a soft spot underneath.

'I'm frightened of what I shall find . . . what is he going to say?' (Very long pause.) 'He says, "What you are seeking lies in the darkness." He says, "The darkness has to be kept soft so that it can be worked with like clay, not allowed to go hard so that it binds."'

'He says that his outer covering appears to people who approach according to the way in which they are seeing the darkness. If they see it positively then he would appear as a warm whole rather than with a spiny covering outside.

'He says he is not really blind. He appeared to be blind because he only sees within, and yet he sees within so truly that it shows what is without as well . . . No more.'

We had a brief final meditation just to give thanks for this progress and to seal the centres; then, quite outside our time, Ruth had this flash:

'The black eagle had grown smaller; the white eagle had grown to the same size as the black one; and they both flew out of the top of the cage which is now open. They flew to opposite sides of the sun and came into the centre of the sun from opposite sides, and were fused into one golden eagle in the heart of the sun.'

*   *   *   *   *

On March 3rd I had a letter from Ruth to say that Gildas was back and that she was overjoyed. Later she wrote that, even so, she was still in the depths and hopelessly stuck with the inner images. 'Gildas has explained little. He is *there*, and a great comfort, but apparently I have to work very much of this out without his help.'

During this period, we were meeting only for a few hours on one day each month, at my home. At our next two meetings, in March and April, there was so much urgency in view of the rapidly expanding mailing list, the accumulation of questions for Gildas, and the need for more teachings, that—apart from a very little work—the inner journey was neglected. Ruth told me, however, that everything was dark and cold, and that the darkness was of a quality blacker and denser than she had ever experienced before. It looked as though a yet deeper level had to be faced and explored.

By early June, Ruth was finding it very difficult to dredge up feelings and images and to communicate in words at all. However, in a conversation recorded on tape, we spoke about Gildas' absence from January to March.

'What was the reason for it? Did he say?'

'Yes . . . About eighteen months ago I was asked whether I wanted to go on to another initiation which would take quite a long time to prepare for. And I said Yes . . . and apparently

Gildas was told that if he wanted to be my guide right through this, *he* would have to go through another initiation. Otherwise, he could still be with me but not so much *as* my guide. And that was why he went away—for this initiation—and part of his test was doing it, and part of mine was being on my own.'

'And he wasn't allowed to tell you beforehand?'

'No.'

'That must have been hard for him as well as for you.'

'In fact, he didn't *know* just when it would be.'

'Didn't he? So he is subject to these time troubles as well as we are.'

'Yes.'

'And your own darkness—ever since Christmas—has this any relation to his initiation?'

'He said that some of it was a reflection from what he had to go through to achieve it.'

'Quite, because you and he are the same person in a way?'

'Yes.'

'I can see that ... and it makes it more bearable, doesn't it?'

'Yes, much more.'

I asked if it were in order to send Gildas my heartfelt congratulations, and then asked Ruth, 'You don't know anything about yours, yet?'

'Not yet, no. This is what some of the blackness is. This is part of it. But before I can go any further I just have to learn this thing: that the inner and the outer are the same.'

*　　*　　*　　*　　*

At our next meeting, at the end of June, Ruth reported that she had started to fall down a very dark shaft; the blackness became thicker and denser and her main problem was that she could not take a breath and felt she would suffocate. We barely had time to work on this problem, but she agreed to keep in touch by writing down the journey as it took place.

Gildas, appealed to for advice, said that her physical symptoms (constant sore throat and conjunctivitis) were part of a phase and that any form of spiritual healing would help. As far as the inner journey was concerned, he told us just to follow the pattern; the more time given to working on it, the more quickly it would come through (in our time). To some extent, he said, physical symptoms and inner work go hand in hand. The outer aspect should not be too severe.

During music (Beethoven) Ruth had the following meditation:

'I saw two doves, one black with gold feet and a silver beak, the other white with silver feet and a gold beak. On each wingtip the birds had an eye of many colours. I was not exactly "with" them, but I could follow their flight and see what they did. They flew into the rainbow, and went through each colour in all its shades and phases, until finally they emerged beyond the rainbow. There I noticed that the white bird was still reflecting with great beauty all the rainbow colours. The black dove seemed for a moment dull in comparison, but then I realized that it had absorbed all the colours, and, though they were not reflected, they were contained within the bird. The white bird was feminine, the black bird masculine. The birds then went to their nest which was silver, and in it lay a golden egg.'

CHAPTER 15

The Seventh Journey

June to August 1968

By Ruth and Mary

The Left Hand Path (Ruth, from letters written later)

At the bottom of the shaft I was faced with two passages, one to the right, another to the left. Slowly I went along the passage to the left. Progress was painful, breathing getting worse every moment. The air seemed solid, and it seemed to be pressing in on me from all directions. My ribs felt as though they were being crushed by a giant hand. The darkness was blacker than black; my despair deepened with every tiny step. I bent down, intending to crawl, thinking there might be more real air at ground level. The crushing pressure became worse, it was impossible to move forward at all, and I thought I should never find the strength to stand upright again. Slowly I managed to fight against the pressure and stand once more, but the effort exhausted me; I desperately needed air, my whole body felt squeezed and crushed, my head spun and I gave myself up to suffocation and exhaustion, thinking the end of at least a part of me had come. Yet nothing died; I did not even lose consciousness, but a great and terrible blackness descended, so that the former darkness seemed light in comparison. This darkness invaded me both without and within; it entered into me through all the openings of the body, and I was too exhausted to fight against it. I was the darkness, and the darkness was in me, and the process continued until 'I' was no longer; all that existed was this terrible blackness.

Eventually it left me and 'I' was once more, but what time passed is hard to say—moments, minutes, or an eternity? If I had felt pain before, it seemed slight in comparison to what now came to me. Each breath had to be fought for even more, and the inside of my body, where the blackness had been, seemed to have been seared and burned by its hot breath. In all my body, I suddenly realized, only my womb was at peace, and this because within it lay the seed of something which in due course would be created and born. I realized with horror and disgust that this seed had been implanted by that terrible, searing, invading blackness. My womb, essence of femininity, queried not, judged not the source, but was at peace, preparing to carry out harmoniously its essential role.

With the rest of my body in misery, pain and revolt, I struggled slowly on, until suddenly I found there was nothing ahead. It was so black that I could not see, but my feet could feel the end of the rocky path. My misery is such that I no longer care what happens; I step on and begin to fall once more into inky blackness. At least the airlessness has ceased; I fall through rushing currents of air and can breathe again with ease; some of my agony, at least, has ceased.

* * * * *

I fall on and on, the air sometimes unbearably hot, at other times unbearably cold, but at least now it is breatheable. As I fall, I realize that to hate whatever is growing in my womb will give it strength which can be used savagely and destructively. Somehow I must accept, and even love this thing, so that when it is born, though a thing of darkness, it will be acceptable and useable. I become more and more convinced that it is *not* a child that I carry within me.

I reach the end of my fall and a terrible darkness envelopes me. I feel utterly desperate, desolate and despairing. There is nothing—only blackness and a terrible, biting cold.

* * * * *

The inner world is very grim and stuck. This terrible cold is awful, it is difficult to breathe again, not now for lack of air but because my frozen body just works so painfully slowly. It is quite horrid, and this frozen-up feeling is coming through into the outer world; I am finding it *so* difficult to write or communicate at all. Yet it helps to make the effort and your letters have been a real sort of oasis.

More Work on the Journey (Mary)

Clearly, it was high time that some intensive work was done on this situation, but the difficulty was always that of lack of opportunity to be together for long enough.

However, from July 27th to August 3rd we met, together with the rest of the small inner group, at White Lodge, Speldhurst, where the established healing centre and pure atmosphere gave the necessary 'lift', and Ruth's journey began to flow. The day was taken up with group work, and most of Gildas' basic teachings on Wholeness and Healing (subsequently published in *Light*, Spring 1972) came through during this week, but Ruth and I managed to set aside an hour over early tea each morning, even on the last day, for personal work. The following account is a diary of these early morning sessions.

July 28th

After a considerable period of introversion, Ruth drew three diagrams:

1   2   3

She associated:

(1) 'The tight ego, feeling pulled apart by forces. It is afraid of disintegration.

(2) 'If the defences went, it would be like this: they would feed into the centre.

(3) 'A circle containing all, but not yet filled.'

July 29th

Ruth felt more relaxed and began to 'unwind'. 'The ice is beginning to melt.'

Gildas had a message to give:

'That into which you must now go forward you will find painful, but, as you go, try these things:

'To see your own actions with understanding and compassion; to remember that I have already seen all, and yet still love and respect you dearly.'

Ruth then let herself go into the experience, speaking very quietly as if from far away, and at long intervals. I took down what she said.

'The ice is melting quite quickly and, as it melts, it is as if I am re-living this part of me and seeing again the things that I did...

'It's going quite fast... I seem to have got outside the time dimension altogether... seeing things that happened over a long time very quickly... Do you want details? They are pretty horrible.

'It is mostly to do with Black Magic, mainly in Atlantis. No, I was not a priestess, I was not incarnate at all. I taught people how to invoke the dark forces, how to use their bodies so that the dark forces could enter into them and be used for power. There was a weak-minded priest who had a certain amount of power; he had been trained for the light but he wanted to find easier ways of achieving knowledge and power on the other side. I appeared to him and told him the sort of rituals that would bring about the dark forces and that enabled him to influence other people for his own ends.

'The rituals were quite horrific: they were done mostly through sex with very young girls. This man had sex with girls;

so did others—people he had in his power—half-idiots who were given very strong aphrodisiacs. The girls were stretched out and made naked on a stone in an old temple of the light. These girls were just raped over and over again by the priests and others until they were driven out of their bodies in such a way that the messages they brought came from the dark forces. They were driven quite out of their minds. They were not just used once and then killed; they were kept, hardly fed, their bodies weakened and used again. When they got completely beyond bringing back anything, they were just allowed to starve—not even a merciful end. Their bodies were given as the only food to others in his power, so they were forced to be cannibals as well.

'Eventually this temple, which was once for the light, became a very powerful force for the darkness, and a lot of evil people were drawn to it. There were great orgies and sacrificing of children—several different rituals depending on the age of the child. One that invoked a lot of power was the sacrifice of a small baby; they just cut its throat and held a sort of travesty of what we would call a communion service, drinking its blood. They worshipped an enormous golden phallus and had frightful orgies, not only amongst themselves but they also enslaved innocent people and used them. Older children were often tortured before they were sacrificed. By these methods they could get for themselves such power that they (the priests) could perform all sorts of miracles, but they always used this power over others for the darkness. They could see into the future how to gain power and wealth for themselves. They could perform even more powerful magic if they could get for their use in their orgies girls who were willing. I would appear in dreams to girls and persuade them that they could achieve power, riches, and fame by dedicating themselves in service to this temple but these things were never fulfilled because they were treated just like the others. They used all sorts of ways of terrifying people to drive them to the states where the evil could enter into them so that they became mad, left their bodies and were possessed by something evil. They used snakes a lot; the poison from snakes was in some of the filth they ate. They knew how to milk poison from a snake. They would terrify people by throwing them into a cage with these snakes, though in actual fact the snakes could do no harm because they had had their poison taken. They would hold people over a pool where there were crocodiles— ever nearer to the water so that they didn't know if they were going to be thrown in or not. They would give them drugs to heighten their sexual desire to such a point that when it wasn't fulfilled they went crazy, and they would prevent them fulfilling it.'

July 30th

In the night Ruth had a dream :

'After this interlude between lives was over and I began to go towards the light again, I incarnated with all the powers that I had developed in the past in the temples of light very much with me. I think it was in Egypt. I was in the temple; there was a war on, and the temple was invaded. The priest whom I had in- fluenced from the other side by black magic was there, in the invading army, and I was used as those girls had been used, and tortured. I had so much power from past lives that it was an enormous struggle before I would leave my body. Eventually I just died, and did not act as a medium for them. The torture was rape; they strapped sharp things on to themselves and then stuck them up me.'

We continued working :

'With all this, the ice has melted, and I just have this terrible pain of *feeling*—it's quite wordless. It is still very dark, but warm. The pain is in the heart centre and is rhythmic; it comes up to a climax and then fades again. It has to come to a real climax . . . the main difficulty is not to fight against it with tension . . .' (A pause while she allowed the climax to occur.)

'Most of it has come and gone now . . . it's a bit like that blackness when I had to lose myself in it . . . right at the very height of it I had the most marvellous healing light from Gildas coming right down into the darkness—just after the final pain— perfectly timed . . .

'Now I'm beginning to gather myself up and think about go- ing on. It's still very, very dark; I can't see anything at all. Breathing is easier. At least it's not cold now, nor unpleasantly hot ... I've come to the end of something, there's no floor ahead at all ... the wall goes on, on the left. I can see just a little bit ... there's a very narrow ledge following the wall round, then another very great drop. I'll go round the ledge and see ... There's nothing on the other side, the ledge just goes right round and comes back. There's nothing but to drop ... All this is so much easier with this new peace I've got inside ... (Allowed herself to drop.)

'It's getting hotter ... it's growing lighter, but this sort of light is almost worse than the darkness—a sort of evil green light ... steam and vapours rising. The sides of the shaft are slimy and horrid. There are all sorts of ghastly slimy creatures clinging to them. And the shaft is getting narrower so that I can hardly avoid touching the sides. And now it is absolutely scorching hot and an awful sickly smell with all these vapours, and these creatures are sort of half-dead, and yet they are still alive ... and the heat is strange in a way, it's hot *and* cold. One feels the heat, but cold inside ... I'm beginning to feel very heavy, almost as though my inside is turning to stone, and I'm falling very slowly ... going down through clouds of sulphur and again I can't breathe—or I can, but every breath burns.'

July 31st (Crisis day and turning point)

'Awful panic ... it's about this place. I'm still going down with these horrid creatures on the sides. It gets narrower and narrower so that I'm forced to touch them. They are life, which is revolting. When I touch them I seem to get an awful shock right through me. When they touch me they give a horrid scream and die ...

'Below me the shaft is just blocked by these creatures. This screaming and death seem to take something from me, as if something of me dies with them. But they smell absolutely awful ... (long pause).

'I've got through. I seem to have taken something of them into me. I seem to be like them, complete evil: power for its own sake. They are fairly small and yet they radiate this green evil ... they want to make all things like them; nothing should be that

they don't possess. There's a complete lack of *being* in a way—
they kill, murder or torture; they only want anything to be or to
live on *their* terms.'

Later in the morning we sat together for a while in the chapel.
Afterwards Ruth told me : 'I went back into all this, and at first
I felt it wrong to do it in the chapel, but I was told it was all
right, just to let it come. And I went on falling in this place; the
shaft was wider again; there were no more creatures on the
sides, but still there was this awful light of evil and the sulphur.
It was getting hotter and there seemed to be terror in the air.
There was nothing to do except go on, because the shaft was now
so wide that I was falling very fast; there was no chance of
catching a foothold on the sides to stop. The last part was this
awful panic again.'

Ruth felt very faint and ill all day; she had identified with
the evil creatures and could not bear to be touched. In the
afternoon she even felt suicidal.

Between tea and supper she went with one of the group to
Speldhurst Church (dedicated to St. Mary the Virgin) where
she had a wonderful vision : she felt completely accepted (yet not
touched) by the Divine Mother whom she saw there. This had
the effect of completely stopping her former wish *not to be*; she
now wanted to live and *to be* 'to the glory', even if to only a
very small part of it. Before tea, she had sprained her ankle
slightly, and it seemed to her that a part of her test was the long
hilly walk to the church and back; the ankle was much better
when she returned.

August 1st

Even before we met over early tea, Ruth had done some work.
She reported :

'Still this panic . . . still going down, down, down. Then I
began to slow down and I came into a sort of cave, an enormous
cavern. In this cavern is the most gigantic lizard-creature, whose
scales are made of green evil light. He is quite enormous; he
lives in this cave. In a way he can't move, he's grown so big. My
first fears were that he would attack or destroy me, but he's not

destructive in that way. The only way through is to creep beneath him, and I did wriggle along. At one point I had the most awful phantasy that I should be squashed—absorbed into him in a way. Then I got to the end of his body, and there was a gigantic tail, going down, which I have to follow wherever it goes.'

During our usual early morning hour, she continued:

'At first the space occupied by the tail is quite large and I can go along beside it without touching it, then it begins to get narrower and darker, so that I just have to touch the tail in order to find the way. All the time I keep wanting to go back . . .

'Now it's quite dark except for a faint glimmer of green from the tail, and I can see that it has grown into the ground and has to be set free. I can't see how this can be done. It's useless to dig because there's nowhere to put anything that's dug away . . .'

I asked, 'Is it earth or rock in which the tail is embedded?'

'I don't know . . . It's a sort of volcanic lava. I want to go back, but he's still growing so there's no way of going back. Complete panic now . . .' (long pause.)

'There's the jewel which I always have with me, and when the scales are held in the light of the jewel, then the volcanic lava recedes, but it involves going right round the tail and touching every bit of it. I find it very difficult to touch it at all. This thing itself doesn't like to be touched, especially by the light of this jewel which is warm; it corresponds to something in me which is cold and hard and does not want to have to feel.'

August 2nd

'I've got to the end of the tail. At the very tip . . . just a tiny little spot on the very tip was made of "inert gold", and when the light of the jewel shone on it, the whole monster and tail and everything just shrank, and what was left was just a small black lizard with the most beautiful golden tail. He has all the room to move now and can scuttle around, and the gold from his tail lights the cave, so he's not in the dark any more. The gold is not now inert, it's been activated.

'The volcanic lava has completely gone in this process of

activating the gold. And the passage is going pretty steeply downwards still ... Help! ... Oh, now there are steps, slippery because of water running down. Still the green light and the fumes
of sulphur. And I'm very, very "preggy"!

'Now there are a lot of snakes, red ones ... they are hot
snakes. They don't bite, they crawl all over me, then they go on
up the stairs. I've gone terribly cold, and they are hot as they
crawl over me. It's the most awful sensation ... it has set off a
whole lot of negative emotions, all wrapped up together : anger
and hate and fear and destruction.'

August 3rd

'Snakes ... I hate them ... I start going down, rather slowly
because of these snakes that keep coming ... Now I can see the
place that they are coming from; it's a horrid place. I don't quite
know why it fills me with such horror. It's quite small, like a
little hole in the side of the shaft—just about enough room for
the snakes to wriggle in and out, one or two at a time. Further
down this hole they go down a sort of passage-way to a bigger
place where they stay, like a rabbit-burrow. When they are there
they are all tied up together in a knot. The light there is a negative red, comparable to the negative green ...

'Most of the snakes have now gone up the shaft, but there's
a red egg left. It contains the essence of all my horror about this
place and I have to crack it ... I can't do any more.'

Between the week at Speldhurst and our week together at
Ruth's home (August 13th to 20th), Ruth was haunted by dreams
of this egg. At her home we followed the same programme as
before, giving the first hour of the morning to the journey work.

August 15th

'I don't know how to crack it; it's got a very tough skin ...'
(long pause.)

'I want to communicate this but I can't, it's wordless ... I
used the jewel; it melted the skin, just at one end, then it came
off in strips, and on the inside of the skin there was a great
quantity of light which was absolutely unbearable in this place
... And then there are all these terrible sensations, as if I went

through all the emotions in every way that they appear, experiencing each one in its coldest aspect right through to its hottest.

'First came *fear*, at first cold, then hot—a different type of panic. With icy cold panic you feel frozen, but the hot panic has all the essence of destruction in it. The bit that was experiencing all this was something very tiny, soft, just sort of one cell; it's the bit that can't be destroyed and it can't destroy either. It can't destroy itself, and it is all that's there, and yet it is still vulnerable and still feels it all. At this point there *isn't* any unconscious.

'After the fear, there was *anger*, first cold, then hot. The cold is actually more destructive than the hot. This (the cold) almost *did* threaten to destroy the essence because it's so shutting-out of life. Yet now I'm fighting to *be*. So, in a way, it's a comfort to know there isn't any way to achieve unconsciousness.

'And now there's *hate*, similar to anger. Cold hate is more destructive. This one cell is all there is, so it can't turn the hate outward; it's just experiencing the essence. Cold hate is just a great suffocating weight, probably the most negative experience that we have. In the hot phase there's something more positive; it has something of destruction in it and yet hasn't that which denies its own destructive quality, so that it doesn't destroy outside itself so much as burn itself up.

'And now there's *despair* ... that's the most wordless of the lot ... The worst phase is the hot one because you are still feeling and it is more painful. It's probably the more acute phase of despair but it is more difficult to get rid of. Cold despair is not feeling. That's as far as I got.'

Ruth felt much more positive after this intense introversion, and she looked a bit like a new-born cell. I found myself saying, 'Hullo! Hullo, little cell!'

August 16th

(After a very long period of withdrawal):

'Then came *sorrow*, then *compassion*, and finally *love*, but all difficult to put into words. Love has so many forms. The last bit of love was being part of all the love there is. And then this little thing began to take in some of the light inside the shell, and it changed into a tiny golden seed; and it began to beat, and I began to beat with it, and it was taken into me and I was taken into it. No separation. Then I went back to the main shaft, and I am still going down. And I'm in pain because the birth is beginning and it is very painful.'

August 17th

'I'm still going down. It's very hot. I want to go slowly but there's something pressing down on me from above making me go quickly. I want to be in rhythm with this birth process, but the pressure hurries me along. It's horrid because of this conflict of rhythm.

'It's dark ... there's a roaring noise ... I'm not going down any more; I'm going along a narrow passage-way. It's not so hot but the walls are damp and the atmosphere of evil is awful.

'There's a place, a sort of great cavern, and coming into it is a great waterfall. This was the roaring noise. And it's the water of evil. There are people working here, channelling this water into pipe-lines. As they work with the water, so they touch it—come into contact with it—and any part of them that isn't completely dedicated to evil shrivels and dies so that they are half-skeletons, but some are so completely evil that they are just horrid, worse than the half-skeletons.

'I must go through this place but with light and strength from somewhere so that I shan't be touched by the water at all. Gildas is here. He's giving me a very lovely cloak of light, but he also says that before I step into this place I have to be completely centred, completely one-pointed towards the light, otherwise all desire to dabble in evil and black magic will be found out and serve to keep me here. Then he says I can throw off this old fascination, it's not really part of me. But there must still be compassion. Anything negative here will call forth an answering chord in this place ...'

At this point, I did a major invocation of all the powers of the light which I knew, and had a wonderful response with some potent symbols. After a very long period of introversion, Ruth continued:

'I went straight through, and right through the waterfall to

the other side quite safely, in a way bringing light into this place
—a terrible and painful experience. On the other side of the
waterfall the passageway is still going along, level. Gildas has
gone, and has taken with him this light cloak, and I'm dressed
in something quite dark which is more protective in a way . . .
Enough for this morning!'

Ruth then recalled that, in a still earlier morning exercise
with Gildas, she had been trained in concentrating on, and in
being, light.

August 18th (Sunday)

Ruth started by feeling great panic, but again we invoked all
the forces of light. There was a very long period of complete
silence—lasting three-quarters of an hour, while she worked in
the inner world. Then she spoke :

'I can't really believe it, but I've come right through!'

'I went along the passage; I had on this cloak, and I realized
that although it was dark on the outside, it was lined with the
most brilliant light. There was this awful green evil light, and
clouds of sulphur, and an awful roaring again. Then I came to a
place where the passage opened out like a gallery going round
a great pit; it was terribly, terribly hot and difficult to breathe
because of the sulphur. In the pit burned the fires of hell.

'I had to go down into them, and in the midst of the fire the
thing that I'd been carrying in my womb was born. It was a
dark jewel, very very dark and yet giving out the most intense
light so that even the fires of hell couldn't withstand it and they
died down. Then I saw some steps going upwards and now I
was carrying the jewel underneath the cloak. I went up the steps
into the presence of the Devil. There was a sort of battle of will,
as if I were searched right through for any chink in the armour
of light so that I could in some way be enslaved in evil again.
It was a terribly painful process, almost as though all my flesh
were stripped away to the insides of my bones; I just kept thinking of Gildas and the light. And when the Devil realized that he
had no way of getting power over me, I was allowed to turn and
go towards the way out of his den which was guarded by two
fearsome creatures, dragon-like but worse than dragons. They

were controlled by the will of Satan. And as I went to go past them, fairly high up and to the right of the exit there was a sort of hollow, and I knew that this dark jewel had to be left there. The powers in this place didn't want it left. I had the most terrific help at that moment, and I was able to do it and walk out without being challenged by the guardians of the gateway. And then I went upwards through a very dark passage-way not really realizing that it was all over, exhausted and in pain and not knowing how to go one step further. I just said, "I can't go any further." And Divine Mother came and said, "You don't have to; nobody has to go beyond what they can do." Then Gildas came, and many other lovely presences, and in their strength I was taken up a golden stairway through a golden gateway to a place of healing and light. That was it.'

* * * * *

The Temple of Healing (Ruth)

Mary commented that we had worked so hard in sharing and recording the dark and painful aspects of all the journeys, it would be good to have at least one hour spent in capturing the happier experiences in lighter realms. So, on the following morning I gave her this description :

It's absolutely fascinating. This is a place of colour-healing, a sort of temple. There's a process that is gone through, and Gildas is showing me the whole process, although a part of me is still there experiencing only part of it. (I am being given blue.)

They said there were many of these places, and people come to them in sleep; also people are brought here when they have died.

First of all people are brought into a reception-place and washed, bathed in water charged with light. Then they lie on a couch and have pure light shone on to and around them. Then they are very carefully looked at—all the chakras examined—to see what sort of therapy they need. All is done through colour in this place, and there are different places for the different colours—different little rooms. You go first to one, and when they think you are ready you go on to the next, and the body gets the treatment that has been prescribed for it. The intensity is very carefully calculated. The patients are observed the whole time, so that if quite a strong intensity of any one colour is needed, they start it off very gently and when they see it is accepted they step it up.

Many people wonder where they are and try to struggle against it, so they just send that struggling part of them away, and they probably have a nice dream whilst they are offered treatment.

Then there's a place where people go before they have to return; it is a place of transition where they see things with which they are familiar, so as to help them to return more gently.

Mary asked, 'Is it a good thing before sleep to visualize yourself in such a temple?'

I replied, 'Yes, although in this particular case the healing is given to those who need it and who are spiritually awakened. It would definitely help to do that. Gildas says there are many of these places where there is music as well.'

Later in the morning, in meditation, I had a profound and very real experience in which I *knew* that all things were one. This, at the time, I found impossible to express in speech, but later on I attempted it in writing:

In God are all things present, yet the essence of God transcends all things. This divine essence surpasses the highest realms of light and sees even beyond and below the utmost depths of evil. None can know of Infinity save this essence of God, yet since all that is made is of this essence, so are all contained within the infinite vision of the essential God; all are a part of it, and collectively the experience of it.

All things are one: inner and outer, height and depth. There is but one experience, and when we are at one with it all burdens are removed, all conflicts resolved. We are what we are, and know tranquillity and peace of spirit in the experience of being.

CHAPTER 16

Prelude to Initiation

Towards the end of the time which I spent in the healing temple, I was prepared in meditation, and rest, and with pure gentle white light, for the moment when I should go with Gildas to the Initiation Temple.

My heart was very full at this time. I was not exactly apprehensive about the initiation, but I realized that I was going forward into an experience of great significance, and yet one which in this life I should probably never fully understand. Gildas told me that I must be sure that I went forward purely by my own true inclination; he advised me to search my being in order to be sure of this inclination; he said that I must find out whether there was any feeling of *unconscious* persuasion, whether I was prepared to go on to please *him*, or perhaps through some feeling of inevitability. Then he left me alone, in a place of peace and light, where, searching within, having admitted and laid aside many reasons why I wished to go on, I came face to face with my own inner truth, and knew unshakeably that the path which I was preparing to tread was my true path. I recognized that the decision to go on was mine alone, and in this moment of truth and vision I realized, somehow, something of what lay ahead : with the Seventh Journey behind me, the actual experience of initiation I felt sure would be supremely positive and joyful—but what of the return? To accept initiation of this kind would mean also to accept a 'return' with heightened sensitivity to an already difficult environment. Further, it would probably mean a greater degree of commitment : the acceptance of the necessity to learn, perhaps painfully, many more lessons before this present life-experience ends. And yet there came also the knowledge that because of the initiation there would come a deep abiding joy and strength which even at life's lowest ebb would never again be overshadowed. I knew also that none of any individual's experiences of this kind was for the self alone but for humanity, the world, the light; and I was ready to go forward by true inclination and, if necessary, alone. Though it means that sometimes we are asked to reach this point of realization and decision, we are seldom in fact asked to go alone, and at this moment Gildas—full of joy—was with me, and as we stood there together I was aware of an immense band of helpers unfailingly at hand.

No further preparation was necessary, and together, on a shaft of pure white light, we approached the place of initiation . . .

It seemed as though we were approaching a great sun or star of coloured light; its brilliance and colour are quite indescribable since every hue in its every aspect is present here, and many of the colours we cannot in our earth bodies perceive as yet. Into this brilliance we seemed to be absorbed and integrated, so that we were one with it, and yet not lost in it—still separate experiencing entities and yet part of and in harmony with this wondrous source of light and colour. We seemed to be drawn into the centre of this source, and here I became aware—as I was to be aware throughout the whole initiation experience—of the synthesis of opposites, and of the great nothingness which yet contains all things, and to feel a great sense of 'not being' which is completely positive and contains both the essence and the totality of being. Here was colour in almost unbearable intensity and yet there was no colour, for it was beyond all experience of colour. All things were present, yet not present, for this was an experience beyond experience.

From this experience we seemed somehow to be drawn into the actual temple of initiation. At first I saw the form of this to be hexagonal—in fact made up of many hexagons and also of many six-pointed stars—stars within hexagons, hexagons within stars—the whole flooded with ever-moving, ever-changing light of all colours. There was indescribable music which seemed borne upon the waves of light, and the most wonderful perfume which I seemed not to inhale but to experience right through my body. Now time stood still; life on the material plane continued but this other part of me in timeless ecstasy was allowed to follow these glorious paths. It is *so* hard to commit any of this composite experience to words and paper, but perhaps some chord of experience and knowledge in the reader will be awakened, and the imagination and spirit will be enabled to go beyond mere words, and to touch, if only for a moment, something of that supreme state to which one day we shall perhaps all have conscious access.

I stood within this wondrous temple formed of light, and gradually I began to realize that, though here I saw the symbolism and form which are the marks of my present spiritual path, this place was all things to all men—the place where all paths must meet and the jewel of truth is found. It is the place where all forms and symbols are one, and yet, going beyond form and symbolism, it is formless and devoid of symbols. With this realization came a great peace; all movement of light, all music, all perfume ceased; a pure white light of magnificent intensity shone upon me, and on a vibration of love and joy my Great Teacher stood before me, both hands raised in blessing. I knelt before him, but he took my hands in his and raised me up; as our eyes met, I felt myself drawn into his aura and being, so that a constant flow of communication took place between us. At each step I understood the significance of what was happening because of this communion between this Great Teacher and myself. It was thus, within his protection, and constantly yet wordlessly taught by him, with Gildas near at hand, that I experienced the rituals of initiation.